Supporting FinTech Innovation in the Czech Republic

REGULATORY SANDBOX DESIGN CONSIDERATIONS

OECD
BETTER POLICIES FOR BETTER LIVES

Please cite this publication as:
OECD (2023), *Supporting FinTech Innovation in the Czech Republic: Regulatory Sandbox Design Considerations*, OECD Publishing, Paris, https://doi.org/10.1787/081a005c-en.

ISBN 978-92-64-50424-0 (print)
ISBN 978-92-64-53480-3 (pdf)
ISBN 978-92-64-42855-3 (HTML)
ISBN 978-92-64-63304-9 (epub)

Photo credits: Cover © monsitj/Getty Images.

Corrigenda to OECD publications may be found on line at: www.oecd.org/about/publishing/corrigenda.htm.

Foreword

FinTech innovation has the potential to drive productivity gains, enhance economic growth, encourage innovation that spurs job creation and improves the quality and diversity of financial services. It can promote financial inclusion for the underserved or underbanked parts of the population, such as SMEs without collateral or prior credit history, or citizens in remote areas of the country. Data is at the core of FinTech financial applications. The provision of many such services is enabled by financial innovations where data usage is a cornerstone. Fostering FinTech innovation can strengthen competition in the market, while at the same time allowing the penetration in international markets.

The innovative nature of FinTech applications leads to a perceived uncertainty by both market participants and regulatory and supervisory authorities about the existence and/or applicability of relevant regulatory/supervisory frameworks. Such uncertainty hinders the full exploitation of the benefits of financial innovation. This highlights the benefit of regulatory sandboxes for the entire ecosystem. In this regard, sandboxes and other innovation facilitator arrangements are critical as they allow small-scale testing of innovation in a controlled environment supervised by the competent authorities, allowing engagement in a constructive dialogue with supervisory and regulatory authorities.

Against this backdrop, a technical support Project has been launched in May 2022, funded by the European Union via the Technical Support Instrument (TSI) and in co-operation with the European Commission's Directorate-General for Structural Reform Support (DG REFORM), together with the Organisation for Economic Co-operation and Development (OECD) as the designated implementing partner. The project falls in the area of administrative and regulatory reform and seeks to unlock the potential of FinTech applications and the use of data in financial services in the Czech Republic and to examine the possible establishment of a sandbox in the country to enable FinTech innovation on the basis of data sharing and usage. The development of the FinTech sandbox features as a milestone of the Digital pillar of the Czech National Recovery and Resilience Plan (RRP), which is focused on digital technologies and aims at creating sandboxes in regulated sectors in line with EU priorities. Its successful completion will have a significant importance from political, economic and social perspectives, contributing to the top EU priorities – Green and Digital Transition.

This report summarises the main findings of the individual outputs (See Annex A, Figure 1.A) delivered to the Commission throughout the duration of the Project and provides recommendations on the design of a feasible regulatory sandbox for FinTechs in the Czech Republic. The main findings stem from an analysis of the FinTech market in the Czech Republic and include an overview of the local FinTech ecosystem, the regulatory and supervisory framework that supports it, existing obstacles to FinTech development, and opportunities for the Czech policy makers to address the identified challenges. The main findings support the subsequent recommendations on the design of a feasible Czech regulatory sandbox presented in the report. The recommendations have been developed in close consultation with the Czech Authorities and European Authorities and draw on past experiences of sandbox models in jurisdictions where these have been established (in OECD and non-OECD member countries with a focus on European Union countries).

The Czech FinTech sector is a nascent market, with more than one hundred regulated or unregulated firms as of 2022. These firms operate in areas such as accounting, payments, savings and personal finance, peer-to-peer (P2P) lending and investment crowdfunding, as well as crypto-asset services. A large part of the innovation in the Czech Republic is driven by foreign-owned companies and relies on external funding. the Czech FinTechs operate in a market that is heavily dominated by banks with under-developed capital markets and facing competition from the traditional Czech financial service providers who are also pursuing digitalisation and innovation. Though the Czech population is quick to adopt digitalisation, the Czech consumers are conservative when it comes to investment and borrowing, holding very few financial assets outside of the banking system.

The analysis of gaps and barriers in the Czech FinTech environment suggests that the current dialogue between the Czech Authorities and FinTechs operating in the country is suboptimal. This conclusion is supported by findings from a questionnaire by the OECD circulated among FinTechs. Long authorisation times are reported to be prevailing in the payment service providers sector, a prominent sector of operation among local FinTechs, while the Czech Authorities report low quality of applications in this sector. The lacking communication channels between the Czech Authorities and FinTechs poses a hurdle to the growth of the nascent local FinTech sector, which is also facing additional constraints related to access to funding, shortage in ICT specialists in both sides of the market (Czech authorities and private sector), and an under-developed domestic ecosystem to support FinTech development (including equity markets for such risky investments). FinTechs are at a disadvantage compared to established banks when it comes to access to data. Access to banks customers' data and payment initiation via Application Programming Interfaces (APIs), made available under EU Directive on Payment Services in the Internal Market 2 (PSD2), is the basis for the business model of an important part of FinTechs. However, they have reported technical and operational issues that prevent them from connecting directly to banks' APIs, despite the existence of an industry-led standard for APIs (Czech Standard for Open Banking). Implementation of the standard is voluntary and the actual uptake by incumbent banks remains unclear. FinTechs therefore often resort to costlier solutions of data aggregators' services to access data.

Based on the analysis of the Czech FinTech ecosystem, including regulatory and supervisory practices and business/market conditions, and the comparison of the existing framework against best practices observed in many OECD countries, this report concludes that the establishment of an innovation facilitator could be one of the possible ways to alleviate some of the impediments to FinTech development in the Czech Republic. The recommendations consider the hurdles to FinTech growth related to supervision and regulation that were identified in previous reports produced by this project. It is also recommended that, to the extent feasible, such regulatory sandbox could provide data-sharing when the conditions permit. Also, a data sandbox could be envisaged *without a regulatory component*, and such data sandbox could be outsourced and/or exist outside the Czech Authorities, although even in this case the Czech Authorities would need to participate *inter alia* by means of providing data.

The report does not include any analysis of implications of the local legal framework of the Czech Republic (e.g. administrative law provisions and implications of public law for the implementation). Such legal advice can be obtained by the Czech Authorities from competent parties should they require such an assessment.

The European Commission's Digital Finance Strategy highlights that "Firms should be able to rely on close co-operation between national supervisory innovation facilitators within the European Forum of Innovation Facilitators (EFIF), and a new EU digital finance platform" (Chapter 4.1, European Commission, 2020[122]). The establishment of a regulatory sandbox would allow the Czech innovative companies to participate in cross-border testing in the context of EU initiatives. For example, the EU Digital Finance Platform will allow multi-sandbox testing in two or more regulatory sandboxes in different Member States, facilitating visibility over the tests among national authorities involved in testing.

Although the Fintech contact point of the CNB is participating in the meetings of the European Forum for Innovation Facilitators EFIF, it is a contact point with limited scope. A regulatory sandbox could co-exist with the contact point and would complement the non-binding preliminary guidance provided by the contact point. A regulatory sandbox may also cover for any possible limited capacity of the current contact point considering possible growing FinTech needs due to new or forthcoming EU regulatory frameworks such as Markets in Crypto-assets (MiCA) Regulation, Distributed ledger technology (DLT) pilot regime, Artificial Intelligence (AI) Act proposal, and proposal for a regulation on information accompanying transfers of funds and certain crypto-assets proposals.

The establishment of a financial sector regulatory sandbox is also envisioned within the Component 1.4, Investment 2.5 of the Czech National Recovery and Resilience Plan (RRP), which states, among other things, *"The investment aims to create and operate sandboxes (*i.e. *testing environments) in the financial sector and AI, as tools to support (i) the rapid commercialisation of more accessible, secure, and modern services in these areas; (ii) the creation and growth of innovative firms; and (iii) the digitisation of the economy."*

In particular, the establishment of a facilitator that takes the form of a regulatory sandbox shall allow for the fulfilment of the Milestone 64 – 1.4.2.5 which calls for the establishment of and launch of two regulatory sandboxes in line with EU priorities, one of them in FinTech, by Q4 2023. Within the first year of its operation, the regulatory sandbox would need to support requests by 10 FinTech companies to fulfil Target 65, by Q4 2024. Also, the establishment of the regulatory sandbox could contribute to the fulfilment of other connected milestones and targets of the Czech Republic RRP, such as *1.4.2.3 Pilot co-investment funds for the development of pre-seed investments, strategic technologies and university spin-offs and 1.4.2.4 Internationalisation of start-ups and others* given the innovative nature of eligible participants to the sandbox, and the potential for cross-border testing in co-operation with other EU authorities' regulatory sandboxes or in the context of EU-wide initiatives for cross-border sandbox collaboration.

The establishment of a regulatory sandbox could not only help drive innovation in the market but also within the supervisory and regulatory bodies, given the possible benefits for Czech Authorities from interacting with innovative business models and close observation of the deployment of technology for financial activity.

Acknowledgements

This report has been prepared by Virginia Robano, Ana Sasi-Brodeski and Nayana Satpathy under the supervision of Iota-Kaousar Nassr and with oversight from Fatos Koc and Serdar Çelik within the OECD Directorate for Financial and Enterprise Affairs. Liv Gudmundson and Eva Abbott provided editorial and communication support.

This report is the outcome of a comprehensive consultative process that involved representatives from different stakeholder groups of the Czech FinTech ecosystem over the period April 2022 – May 2023.

The authors gratefully acknowledge valuable input and constructive feedback provided by Alex Ivančo, Lenka Franče Rejzková and Barbora Kochová from the Ministry of Finance of the Czech Republic, Michal Vodrážka and Tomáš Olexa from the Czech National Bank, as well as by Edouard Gomet from the European Commission's Directorate-General for Structural Reform Support.

This Project was funded by the European Union via the Technical Support Instrument (TSI), and implemented by the OECD, in cooperation with the Directorate-General for Structural Reform Support of the European Commission.

The European Commission's Directorate General for Structural Reform Support (DG REFORM) provides support for the preparation and implementation of growth-enhancing administrative and structural reforms by mobilising EU funds and technical expertise, in accordance with the criteria and principles referred to in Article 7(2) of the Regulation (EU) 2017/825. For additional information, please see: https://commission.europa.eu/funding-tenders/find-funding/eu-funding-programmes/technical-support-instrument/technical-support-instrument-tsi_en.

For more on this project please visit https://www.oecd.org/finance/oecd-project-on-data-in-financial-services-in-the-czech-republic.htm.

Table of contents

FIGURES

TABLES

Executive summary

The establishment of a regulatory sandbox by Czech Authorities could foster innovation in the financial sector while allowing supervisors to observe and address emerging risks associated with the deployment of innovative technologies in finance with potential benefits extending to all stakeholders involved. Enhanced communication and interaction with FinTechs through constructive dialogue and customised guidance, clear guidance as to the license category corresponding to the innovative business model, and support in preparing a licensing application are some of the potential benefits for FinTechs who can make more informed decisions, develop tailored strategies, and ensure compliance with applicable regulations. Czech Authorities can enhance their understanding of how such innovative mechanisms may alter the risk profile of certain financial activities, and, in turn, facilitate the development of adequate policy responses, if required. Visible efforts to improve the dialogue between the supervisor and FinTechs can increase the confidence of investors about the viability of local FinTechs and the attractiveness of the domestic FinTech market and signal an openness towards safe innovation in finance, encouraging FinTech start-up activity.

Legal certainty can be enhanced by a regulatory sandbox without the need for bending rules for FinTechs when existing rules and regulations continue to be applied within the framework of such facilitator. Additionally, a regulatory sandbox can benefit supervisors by enabling them to better monitor the activities of FinTechs and ensure compliance with new regulatory frameworks (e,g, Markets in Crypto-assets (MiCA) Regulation, Distributed ledger technology (DLT) pilot regime), while also allowing them to consider any necessary tools and resources needed to ensure proper enforcement of regulations in such new areas.

The recommended design for a Czech regulatory sandbox is based on the feasibility study for its implementation in the Czech Republic and is tailored to the specificities of the Czech ecosystem, considering relevant opportunities and limitations of the domestic environment. The key design recommendations for the Czech Regulatory Sandbox are as follows.

Definition of "innovative financial product": a new or improved financial product, service, or business strategy that leverages novel/emerging technologies to provide innovative/enhanced financial services.

Objectives of the proposed regulatory sandbox for FinTechs: facilitate innovation and speed up productive innovation; promote competition and financial inclusion in the financial sector; facilitate the adoption of new technologies; and attract FinTechs.

Recommended scope: cross-sectoral with no restrictions concerning the sector of activity, if it falls under the remit of the financial authorities, directly or indirectly. In this context, 'indirectly' refers to financial activity that may not fall under the existing definitions of activities requiring a license from Authorities but may still have an impact on the financial sector. Applicants must comply with the eligibility criteria in all cases.

Limits of the testing environment: The recommended structure advises against the provision of any waivers, restricted authorisations or other relaxation of existing applicable rules, which would anyway be against EU rules. It is recommended that a proportional application of existing regulatory and supervisory requirements, as embedded in EU financial services regulation, is used as appropriate, and at the discretion of the supervisor for firms participating in the Czech regulatory sandbox. Such proportionality can apply to the governance process and system and control requirements, board composition; financial soundness; reputation; management experience and track record. Proportionality should be applied on a case-by-case basis by the supervisor, depending on the business model and the applicable rules.

Regulatory and supervisory oversight: The recommendation for the Czech regulatory sandbox to maximise operational benefits and improve the dissemination of regulatory clarity on the one hand, and understanding of business models by the supervisor on the other hand, is to have the sandbox set up by the Authorities. The practice in all EU regulatory sandboxes has been for regulatory sandboxes to be established at the supervisory authority. Since the suggested testing framework will not offer exemptions to participating firms in the sandbox beyond those provided by national and European law, there is therefore no need for legislative changes for the establishment of a regulatory sandbox. The Czech Authorities could establish the regulatory sandbox by an internal act or by designating which posts will be dedicated to co-ordinating its operation within the relevant Authorities.

Standard regulatory vs. data sandbox: The recommendation for the Czech sandbox is to commence with the establishment of the 'standard' regulatory sandbox and, to the extent feasible, provide data-sharing when the conditions allow it. The feasibility of this option will be based on (i) the availability of datasets and ability to make these available; (ii) the capacity of the authorities participating in the regulatory sandbox. It could also be envisaged that a data sandbox without a regulatory component to it could be outsourced and/or be established outside the Czech Authorities, although even in this case the Authorities would need to participate inter alia by means of providing data. The two types of sandboxes, regulatory and data, are not mutually exclusive.

Types of data in the data sandbox: The recommendation about the Czech data sandbox will depend on the feasibility analysis of such endeavour, which, in turn, will depend to a large extent on the datasets that can be made available, taking under consideration legal and technical limitations with respect to companies participating in such facilitator, while it will also depend on the allocation of capacity to operate such a sandbox, both in terms of numbers and in terms of technical skillsets, to allow for its operation.

Synthetic data in the data sandbox: It is recommended to avoid this option at the first stages of development of the data sandbox, unless there is a willingness to deploy important resources, both internally / pre-existing and externally in terms of providers of specialised services that may not be available within the Czech authorities. In the future, depending on the availability of resources and the experience of the sandbox, Czech authorities can consider engaging in a more resource-intensive phase of the data sandbox, involving synthetic datasets.

Participants: Categories of firms that may participate and would find it useful include companies that already have a license but wish to test a new technology and/or business model; companies that do not have the required license within the financial legislation to provide the desired activity; companies where it is uncertain whether the activity requires a license within the financial legislation.

Eligibility criteria: It is recommended that participants in the regulatory sandbox hold the appropriate license for the regulated activity undertaken or are ready to apply for a license in order to have it before the start of the testing phase, if the supervisor deems that the activity falls within the perimeter of regulated financial activity. In case the supervisor deems that a license is not necessary, the Czech Authorities have the discretion to allow the company to perform the testing or not. This could be beneficial for both the Czech Authorities and the service provider, for example, if regulation in this area is being negotiated and co-operation is assessed as beneficial for familiarisation with this type of product.

Authorisation model: Participants are preselected by a special Advisory Board based on enclosed eligibility criteria, which provides a non-binding recommendation. This will then be validated or rejected by the Czech Authorities, and this does not apply to the CNB, as the CNB has no legal basis to issue such a decision. The Authority operating the sandbox would issue a decision regarding the selection upon considering the recommendation of the Advisory Board.

1 Assessment of the Czech FinTech ecosystem

The Czech FinTech sector consists of more than one hundred regulated or unregulated firms operating in a market heavily dominated by banks. Czech consumers embrace digitalisation, yet the current allocation of financial assets is conservative and the capital market is under-developed. Current dialogue between the Czech Authorities and FinTechs may not be optimal and results of the OECD FinTech market questionnaire indicate that regulation is perceived as a key challenge, followed by access to market and funding.

The Czech FinTech ecosystem includes over 100 FinTech companies operating across various segments of activity falling inside as well as outside the regulatory perimeter of supervision. The level of digitalisation is quite high, in the payments service providers sector in particular, which is also a main segment of activity for Czech FinTechs. Findings of the OECD (OECD, 2022[1]) open questionnaire on FinTech activity in the Czech Republic presented at the end of this chapter point to several perceived impediments to FinTech development in the country; these include access to financing, operability of APIs for accessing data, entry barriers by dominant incumbents, and perceived hurdles regarding regulatory issues.

The analysis of the Czech FinTech ecosystem identified several such manifests of regulatory and supervisory hurdles to FinTech growth, such as the "wait and see" approach taken by the supervisors and regulators as opposed to a more proactive approach taken by several other EU Member States; the lack of prioritisation of promoting competition within the financial sector; lengthy licensing procedures for payment institutions; and the cultural differences between the supervisor and the FinTech firms. Additional non-regulatory identified gaps that may impede FinTech growth include banking sector dominance; the lack of sufficient funding sources for Czech SMEs, start-ups included; challenges with regards to data access; dependence on foreign firms for innovation dissemination and the lack of qualified human capital; the low level of business ICT integration; and the conservative investment outlook of the Czech population.

1.1. Nascent local FinTech sector

The development of FinTech activity has followed a pattern of constant growth both globally and domestically in the Czech Republic. The COVID-19 pandemic accelerated and intensified the digitalisation trend that pre-existed in the financial markets and increased both the offer and the demand for innovative FinTech solutions (OECD, 2022[1]). Apart from FinTechs, traditional financial institutions, such as banks and insurance companies, are also active in terms of innovation (OECD, 2022[1]). On the demand side there is openness to new digital financial products, services and solutions, and the business sector is relatively quick in adopting financial services innovations (ICLG, 2021[2]).

1.1.1. Small FinTech sector offering a variety of financial services

There are 113 Czech FinTech companies in the Czech Republic active across a large number of different sectors of regulated and unregulated activity (FinTech Cowboys, 2022[3]). Based on maturity and performance, Czech FinTech firms rank in the bottom third among European countries based on some recent industry studies (McKinsey, 2022[4]). Czech FinTechs mostly provide services in areas such as accounting, payments, personal finance management, peer-to-peer (P2P) lending or crowdfunding (Figure 1.1). Open banking application created on the basis of the PSD2 framework have also become popular. Historically, innovation has consistently been strong in the payment providers sector; in particular around contactless card payments, where the country has been consistently among the top five countries worldwide in the usage of contactless card payments for the half decade (Visa, 2022[5]).

P2P lending platforms represent some of the biggest FinTech companies in the Czech Republic in terms of number of customers or valuation, and crowdfunding as a form of alternative financing[1] is becoming increasingly popular in the country. However, the per capita funding volume of alternative finance platforms in the Czech Republic is among the lowest in Europe (CCAF, 2021[6]). Regulatory changes spanning the crowdfunding sector are underway in the Czech Republic, making these platforms subject to various regulatory requirements under certain conditions. Regulation could increase the attractiveness of this type of investment through crowdfunding platforms (Advokátní deník, 2022[7]).

Figure 1.1. Number of Czech FinTech firms, July 2022

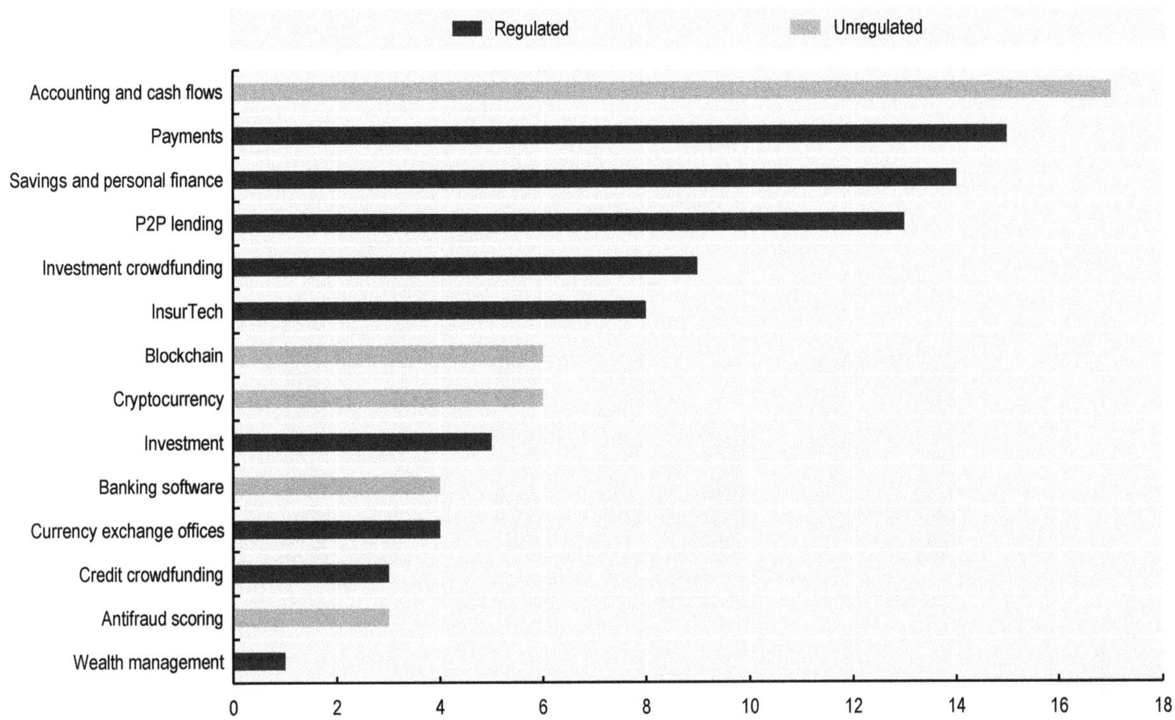

Source: OECD construction based on data from FinTech Cowboys (2022[3]), Fintechová mapa České republiky – jaro 2022: přes 100 fintechů, https://fintechcowboys.cz/fintechova-mapa-ceske-republiky-jaro-2022-pres-100-fintechu/.

1.1.2. Consumer openness to digitalisation drives demand for FinTech activity

Czech citizens are open to the use of digitalised services and products and frequently use financial services through on-line applications for purposes such as paying bills, sending money or viewing account information (World Bank, 2021[8]) (Figure 1.2). They are also accustomed to online purchasing, with the Czech Republic ranking 8th among EU Member States on the share of local consumers shopping online (Ecommerce Europe and EuroCommerce, 2022[9])

Figure 1.2. Use of digital financial services and productive innovative firms in the Czech Republic, as of 2021

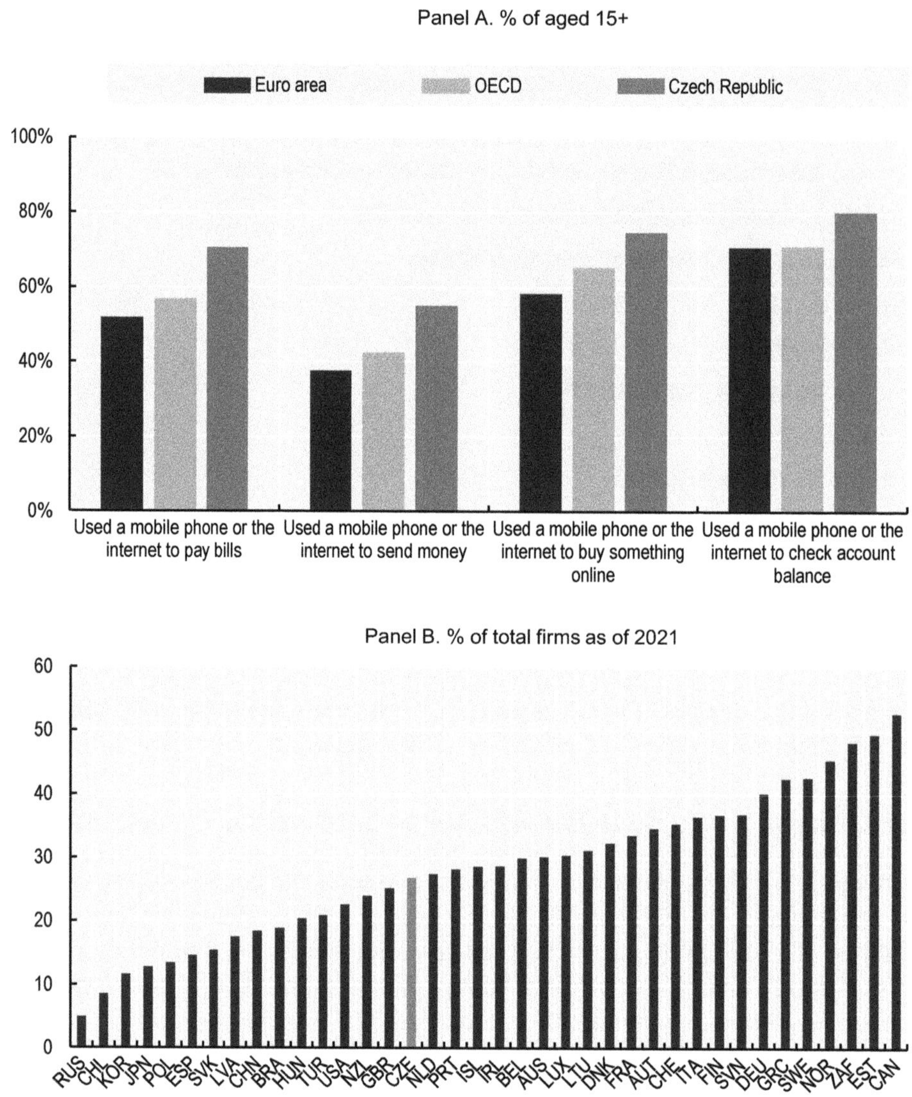

Source: OECD (2022[10]), Business innovation statistics and indicators, https://www.oecd.org/sti/inno-stats.htm#indicators; World Bank (2021[8]), The Global Findex Database 2021, https://www.worldbank.org/en/publication/globalfindex.

1.1.3. Local innovation is driven by foreign-controlled firms and external funding in the presence of local funding constraints

According to the European Innovation Scoreboard for 2022, the Czech Republic is placed among moderate innovator countries with performance at 92.6% of the EU average (European Commission, 2022[11]). The country's performance gap to the EU is, however, narrowing; the Czech Republic has increased its performance twice as fast as the EU average since 2015, and improvement was in particular high from 2021 to 2022 (European Commission, 2022[11]).

Innovative firms in terms of product innovation[2] position the Czech Republic slightly below the average among OECD countries (Figure 1.2). However, the Czech financial and insurance activities are more innovative than the overall business sector, which puts the sector in a leading position of innovation locally, even though it is not usually in that position in other countries (OECD, 2022[10]).

Innovation in the Czech market is currently attributed to foreign-owned firms; the Innovation Strategy of the Czech Republic 2019-30 shows that the majority of innovating enterprises in the Czech Republic were foreign-controlled, mainly large industrial enterprises, in 2016 (R&D&I Council, 2019[12]). Similarly, the share of foreign firms in the Czech Republic is higher among the top productive firms compared to the overall business sector (OECD, 2020[13]). The European Innovation Scoreboard 2022 places the Czech Republic as the third highest in the share of added-value contributed by foreign-controlled enterprises (European Commission, 2022[14]). It should be noted that the presence of foreign firms is not considered to be a sufficient condition for (large-scale) innovation diffusion to take place (OECD, 2020[13]).

Local innovation activities are primary challenged by the lack of sufficient funding, whether from external, internal, or public sources (R&D&I Council, 2019[12]; Czech Statistical Office, 2022[15]). This is despite the goal set up by the Czech Government in 2020 to become an innovation leader within ten years, planning to increase public spending in this area to 2.5% of GDP in 2025 and 3% by 2030 (OECD, 2020[13]). Local enterprises also cite the lack of qualified workers as a major non-financial challenge (Czech Statistical Office, 2022[15]).

Statistics on research and development (R&D) investment at country level show a steady growth of such expenditure in recent years in the Czech Republic, albeit not fast enough to close the gap with EU and OECD countries, in particular as R&D expenditures have accelerated for OECD countries in 2022 (Figure 1.3, LHS). The dependence of innovation on external sources is apparent in R&D investments as well; R&D sourced by the local business sector in the Czech Republic is particularly low compared to EU/OECD countries, while investment coming from abroad is high (Figure 1.3, RSH).

Figure 1.3. Gross domestic expenditure on R&D

Totals of all expenditure on inputs used in performing R&D, in percentage of GDP

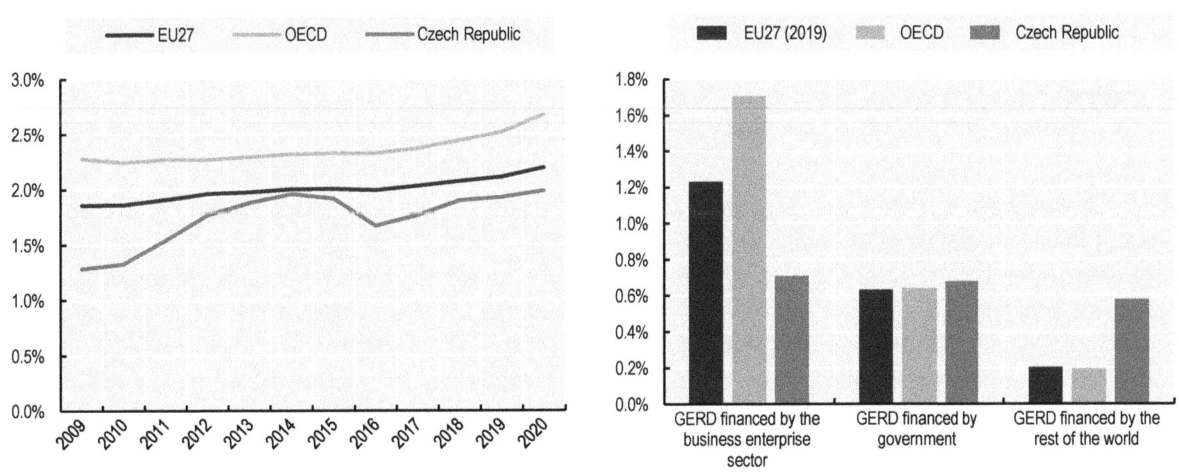

Source: OECD (2022[16]), Science, Technology and Innovation Scoreboard, https://www.oecd.org/sti/scoreboard.htm#publications.

As for information and communication technologies (ICT), Czech enterprises portray higher than EU average presence of their business on-line, corresponding to the high ratio of Czechs performing on-line purchasing. At the same time, less than the EU average share of enterprises are connected to high-speed internet, and fewer enterprises use business software (Czech Statistical Office, 2022[17]). Use of cloud storage for financial data by enterprises, a prerequisite for many innovative financial applications for businesses, is still quite low in the Czech Republic.

1.2. Underdeveloped financial services sector dominated by banks

Czech FinTechs operate in the financial services sector which is dominated by banks in most segments of the financial markets. Small local capital market limits the funding sources of FinTechs but also the variety of services that FinTechs are able to offer to consumers and SMEs in an economy with few existing financial products, and limited options for unbundling financial services. Financial literacy gaps and conservative savings allocation by consumers may limit the adoption of innovative financial services or result in a mismatch between services and consumers and increase the build-up of financial risks.

The assets of the banking system as of March 2022 comprise 85% of the total assets of the domestic (regulated) financial system including pension and investment funds, insurance companies and others (CNB, 2022[18]). Overall credit levels to the private sector in the Czech Republic are low compared to OECD countries, potentially leaving room for growth facilitated by FinTechs (Figure 1.4). In recent years, innovative lending platforms have experienced a boom, especially in the fields of P2P consumer lending and crowdfunding platforms (OECD, 2022[1]).

Figure 1.4. Total credit to the non-financial sector and financial assets of households

Percentage of GDP [LHS], percentage of Net Disposable Income (NDI) [RHS], as of 2020

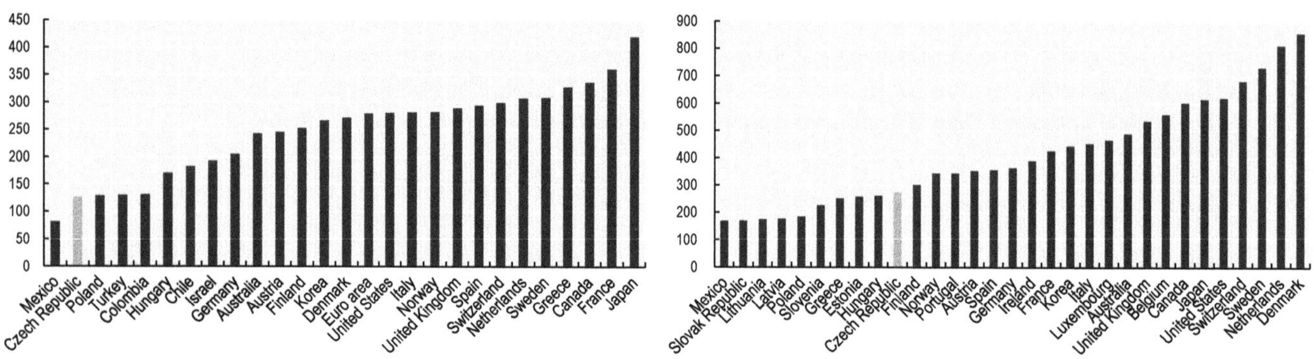

Note: Households includes non-profit institutions serving households (NPISHs)
Source: OECD (2022[16]), Science, Technology and Innovation Scoreboard, https://www.oecd.org/sti/scoreboard.htm#publications.

The Czech Authorities have concluded that the capital market in the Czech Republic is underdeveloped and not sufficiently fulfilling its main function (i.e. to efficiently redistribute free financial resources from savers and investors (households) to entrepreneurs who need to finance their development) (MFCR, 2019[19]). One of the likely reasons for that is that traditional bank financing prevails, while there is also a strong reliance on EU subsidies (but not necessarily in the FinTech sector) (MFCR, 2019[19]). This bias towards bank financing is supported by conservative asset allocation of households, low savings for old age on top of the mandatory pension provisions, low awareness among entrepreneurs of the possibilities of financing business and research through the capital market, and a small range of domestic investment instruments available to retail investors compared to Western Europe (OECD, 2022[1]).

There are no specific regulatory barriers preventing FinTech businesses from co-operating and entering into arrangements with traditional financial services providers, except for the requirements applicable to specific services such as bank outsourcing rules that may be perceived as overly burdensome by the smallest start-ups. However, the traditional financial services providers prefer established, well-known vendors when searching for new digital solutions or improvements to their current offerings, especially in core banking systems, customer relationship management, and trading platforms. However, this is evolving and even though banks have been historically rather reluctant to co-operate with FinTechs, they are starting to focus more on better user experience to ensure greater customer loyalty and more user-friendly, cheaper services to retain clients amid increasing competition in the market driven by the FinTechs. As a result, the level of overall digitalisation of the Czech banking sector and the availability of new innovative solutions or products offered by banks has improved significantly throughout the past decade (OECD, 2022[1]).

1.2.1. Czech consumers channel savings mainly to bank deposits

Over the past decade, financial inclusion of Czech consumers regarding traditional financial products has increased. Current and saving account ownership has grown fast. However, Czechs households stick to a conservative investment outlook – despite a high savings rate within the Czech economy, Czech households rank in the bottom of OECD countries with regard to overall financial assets held (Figure 1.4). More than half of households' savings are held in cash and deposits and only a tiny fraction of savings enters the capital market (MFCR, 2019[19]). Only a small portion of assets is managed outside the banking system; assets under management in pension funds and insurance companies comprised less than 20% of the Czech GDP in 2021 (OECD, 2022[1]).

Compared with OECD countries, Czech households have taken out less loans and hold fewer outstanding mortgages than the average across countries (World Bank, 2021[8]). Few consumers reported using consumer and mortgage debt in 2010 and though this ratio increased somewhat (Figure 1.5), current levels of consumer debt remain relatively low. Supplementary savings have not grown almost at all, and the investment in equity and bonds is extremely low. Given the current setting, there is less business rational for the operation of personal financial advisors or applications for cost comparison at a large scale.

Figure 1.5. Active use of financial products by Czechs

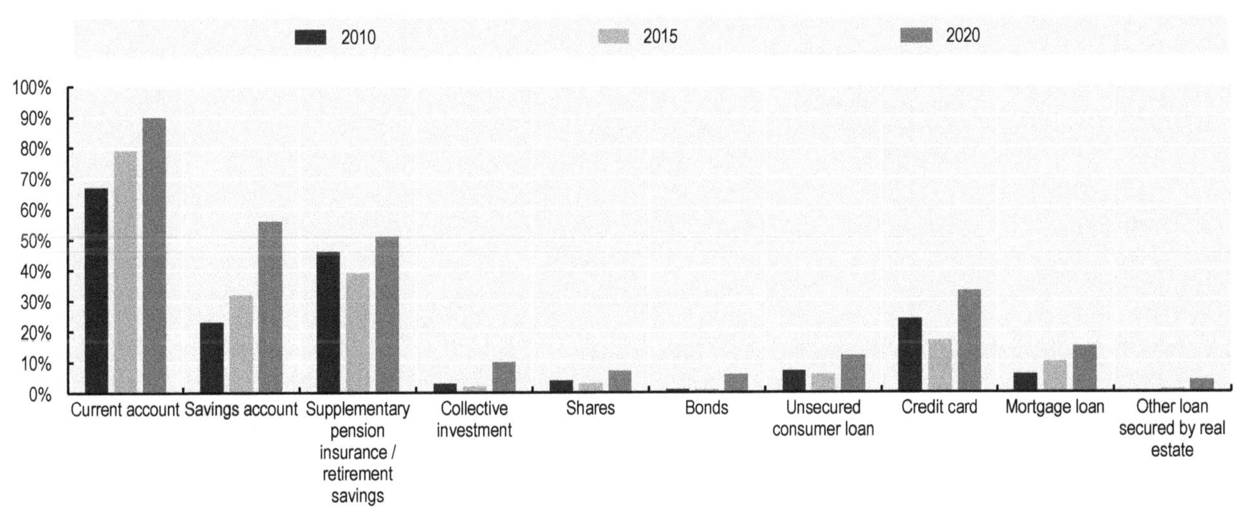

Source: OECD construction based on data from MFCR (2020[20]), Financial Literacy Measurement Results 2020, https://financnigramotnost.mfcr.cz/cs/pro-odborniky/mereni-urovne-financni-gramotnosti/2020/postoje-k-financim-a-chovani-3272/.

1.2.2. Czech SMEs lack sufficient funding sources

There is little Venture Capital (VC) available (Figure 1.6) in the Czech Republic, which, given lack of vibrant equity capital markets, creates a financing gap for early-stage innovative firms in need of capital with high risk tolerance. Lack of equity funding was reiterated by stakeholders from the Czech Republic during discussions and interviews with the OECD in 2020; the availability of finance for innovative start-ups, especially in the very early stages of their life cycle (the so-called proof-of-concept stage), was repeatedly described as problematic (OECD, 2020[13]). Bank credit might not always be accessible for young start-ups without any previous financial history or finished product (OECD, 2020[21]). Banks are generally unwilling to lend to this segment of the enterprise population, while much of the public financial support is not geared to these ventures either (OECD, 2020[13]).

Data from the Survey on the Access to Finance of Enterprises (SAFE) carried out once a year by the European Commission support these findings and suggest that the local bank credit market lacks depth and is less inclusive; among different funding options, Czech SMEs show a low use of bank loans, trade credit and equity to fund their operations and growth. In contrast, the use of credit lines, leasing and hire-purchase and factoring by Czech SMEs is similar to SMEs across the EU. This might indicate that credit sourced at banks is used for ongoing operations of the firm but less for the purpose of investment, business expansion, etc. Moreover, the rejection rate by banks is higher in the Czech Republic compared with the EU average, 16% and 7% respectively. SMEs in other EU countries have a greater ability to receive a partial amount of the loan application or a loan with a high interest rate, with more alternatives for risky borrowers. Equity is rejected almost completely as a potential source of funding for Czech SMEs even up to three years after the START[3] stock trading has been set up [(Figure 1.7), (European Commission, 2021[22])].

Figure 1.6. Venture capital investment by country

Cumulative amounts for 2015-21, in EUR million

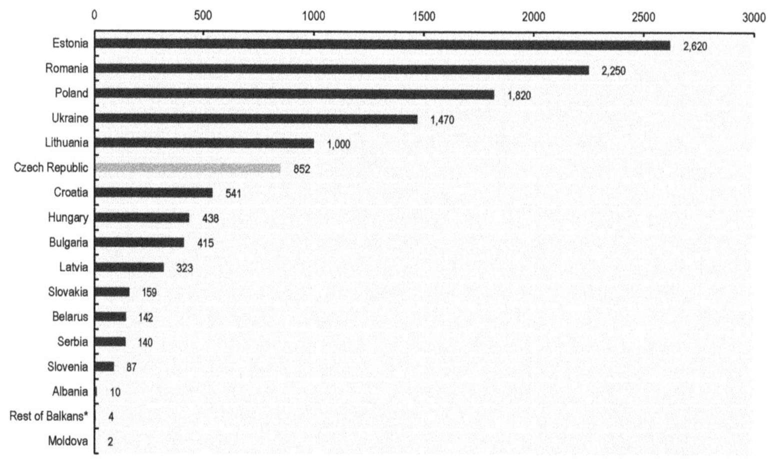

Note: (*) North Macedonia, Kosovo, Montenegro, Bosnia and Herzegovina.
Source: OECD construction based on data from Google for Startups, Atomico and dealroom.co (2021[23]), Coming of age: Central and Eastern European startups, https://dealroom.co/reports/coming-of-age-central-and-eastern-european-startups.

Low credit levels by consumers and SMEs could be the result of a combination of underling factors, and the legal design of the insolvency resolution regime which affects the demand and supply of credit is one of them. Large personal and economic costs associated with distress resolution reduce credit attractivity to consumers and businesses, and such costs also raise the initial price of credit as lenders internalise the possible expected loss. In the comparison of insolvency regimes performed, the Czech Republic scored worst in personal costs to failed entrepreneurs and lack of prevention and streamlining (Mcgowan and Andrews, 2018[24]). In contrast, the Czech Republic scored highest (best) in a third category – barriers to restructuring. This could mean that the design of the court-managed local regime is appropriate, however the "penalty" to failing firms and their entrepreneurs is high and there is inefficiency with regard to early resolution and out-of-court resolution. Regimes should be designed in a way to encourage debtors to take appropriate actions sufficiently early on in their financial difficulties, thereby increasing the chances of a successful restructuring (Mcgowan and Andrews, 2018[24]). A legal framework for preventive restructuring is in discussions at the Czech Republic (Lukas Valusek and Lenka Kučerová, 2022[25]).

Figure 1.7. Sources of financing for SMEs

Percentage of respondents who said yes to the question: "Are the following sources of financing relevant to your firm, that is, have you used them in the past or considered using them in the future?"

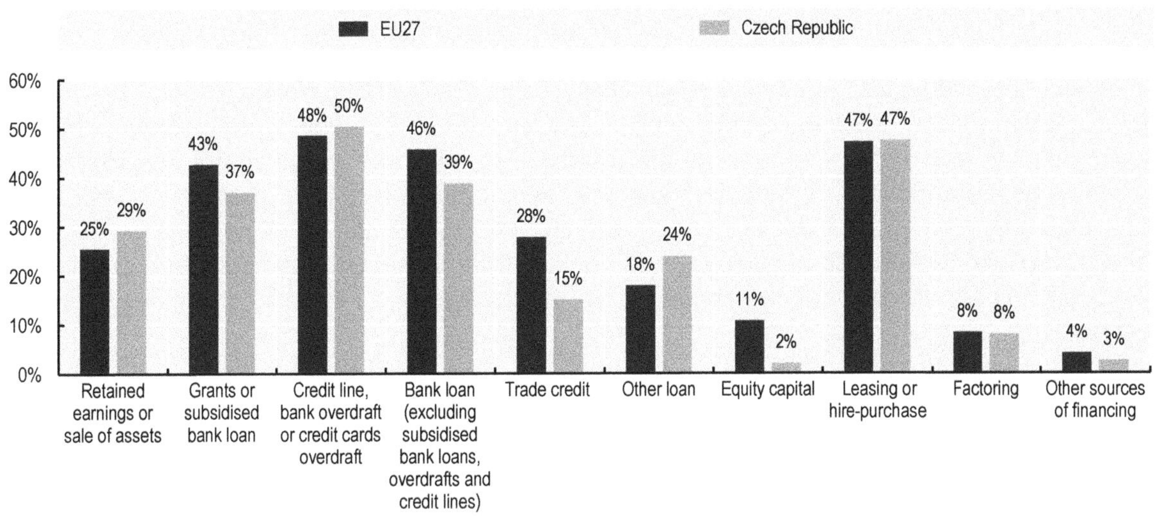

Source: European Commission (2021[22]), Data and surveys – SAFE, https://single-market-economy.ec.europa.eu/access-finance/data-and-surveys-safe_en.

Limited access to foreign financing is another factor possibly underlying the low credit levels of Czech consumers and SMEs. According to the 2019 SBA Fact Sheet of the European Commission, the Czech Republic has the worst performance among EU member states on SME internationalisation. Formalities are relatively cumbersome with limited digitalisation, and SMEs trade less often in goods outside of the EU compared to their counterparts in other EU countries (European Commission, 2019[26]). These observations were echoed by policy makers and other stakeholders, who often reported limited access to foreign markets for most businesses, a few exceptions (of mainly large companies) notwithstanding (OECD, 2020[13]).

Prior research has shown that FinTech lending and the deployment of alternative credit scoring methods could be particularly beneficial in expanding access to credit to underbanked SMEs (OECD, 2022[27]). The MFCR has prepared a National Strategy for Development of the Capital Market in the Czech Republic 2019-23 which was approved by the government and suggests four main actions, each targeted at a different group of stakeholders – households, businesses, market infrastructure and the public sector (OECD, 2022[1]). The strategy suggests an extensive set of policy actions and reforms. All proposed actions include a time frame for execution, however interim assessment regarding the fulfilment of the strategy is not publicly available (MFCR, 2019[19]). One of the implemented actions includes the launch of an informational website called Capital Guide which is intended for SMEs looking for alternatives to bank financing (MFCR and EU, 2022[28]).

1.2.3. Banks hold the data that FinTechs seek to access

Results from the OECD questionnaire shared with Czech FinTechs during the summer of 2022 highlight the central role of data in their business model, the type of data used, and the current difficulties in accessing it as well as limitations of scope. The vast majority of respondents to the questionnaire highlighted the importance of accessing financial data for their business (88%), with APIs being the most frequent venue allowing for data accessibility (88%), demonstrating the important effect that a regulatory obligation for incumbents within the framework of the PSD2 had on the business model of new service providers. More than half (54%) of respondents placed PSD2 regulation as having a high impact on their activity.

Under the PSD2,[4] which went into effect in Czech legislation during 2018 and lays down the legal basis for open banking, banks are required to make their APIs available to payment account information service providers (MFCR, 2017[29]). The PSD2 framework however is not being exploited to its full potential; more than 46% of firms responding to the OECD Questionnaire have had problems accessing customer data from financial intermediaries. Anecdotal evidence by some FinTechs operating in the Czech Republic suggests that FinTechs experience technical issues and other challenges that prevent them from connecting directly to the banks' APIs on a regular basis. FinTechs turn to aggregators to collect the data for them in a centralised way – aggregators and special data purchases from specialised firms are used by more than half of FinTechs (58%). There is currently only a small handful of aggregators operating in the Czech financial market such privately-owned Bank APIs Aggregation Platforms (BAAPI) called Trask and Finbricks. There are also private contracts between banks and FinTechs that allow data sharing (OECD, 2022[1]).

Shortcomings of PSD2 with regard to increased competition in retail payments have been recognised at the EU level (EBA, 2022[30]). The European Commission has been promoting legislation for making data more easily available in a secure way, as part of its long-term strategy on data (European Commission, 2020[31]). The strategy aims at creating a single EU market for data, personal as well as non-personal data, including sensitive business data. Within the scope of this broad strategy, the European Commission has recently proposed legislations on the re-use of publicly held, protected personal and non-personal data that applies to data intermediaries (proposed regulation on harmonised rules on fair access to and use of data) and rules on who can use and access which data and for which purposes (proposed regulation on European data governance) (European Commission, 2022[32]; European Commission, 2022[33]).

More specific to financial data, in 2021, the Commission established an expert group on European financial data space to engage with stakeholders. A year later, a subgroup on open finance was created as open finance is considered to be an integral part of the European financial data space, along with data contained in public disclosures of firms as well as supervisory data (European Commission, 2022[34]). The access and reuse of customer data, with consent, across a range of financial services has already been referred to in the EU Digital Finance Strategy (European Commission, 2020[35]).

In parallel, the Czech Banking Association introduced a Czech Standard for Open banking, which aims at a uniform implementation of the PSD2 API standard in the Czech market. However, the standard is not mandatory, so it is up to the discretion of individual banks to decide whether they want to adhere to the standard or not. One of the most prominent use cases to have evolved from the Open banking standard was the Bank ID implementation: an interface that allows for digital verification of identity owned by nine of the Czech banks.[5] This service seems to be an improvement for consumers, although it may also be valuable for banks to collect data on their customers as to their commercial habits and to verify the data collected within the identification process in public registries, thus reinforcing the advantage of incumbent banks in access and ownership of data, even though direct information on the activity of users within the commercial or governmental site is not visible to the validating bank (OECD, 2022[1]).

1.3. Financial regulation and supervision in the Czech Republic

1.3.1. Unified financial supervision

Financial market activity in the Czech Republic, including FinTech activity, is supervised by the Czech National Bank (CNB) and regulated by the Ministry of Finance of the Czech Republic (MFCR). The CNB is the sole unified supervisory authority for the financial markets in the Czech Republic.[6] The CNB lays down rules in the form of decrees and provisions; it authorises, regulates, supervises and issues penalties for non-compliance with these rules. In co-operation with the Czech Ministry of Finance, which is responsible for the preparation of laws in the financial market area, the CNB participates in the preparation of primary legislation and is responsible for the preparation of secondary legislation (CNB, 2022[36]). The CNB's objective in the area of supervision, as defined by law, is to ensure financial stability and the safe and sound operation of the financial system in the Czech Republic, contributing to achieving its primary objective: price stability. It is worth noting that the CNB has no official mandate with regard to fostering competition in the financial sector (CNB, 2022[37]).

The CNB has historically maintained a technology-neutral approach towards innovation in finance, similar to other OECD countries. According to the CNB, all providers of relevant products and services must comply with those conditions regardless of the innovative aspects of those activities. Nonetheless, in November 2019, the CNB established a FinTech contact point aimed at helping resolve unclear regulatory issues – including licensing and supervisory ones – so as to facilitate compliance with the duties imposed on enquirers by financial market regulations. Opinions of the CNB provided via the contact point do not substitute for authorisations or approvals granted in licensing proceedings and are not binding in any way (CNB, 2022[38]).

1.3.2. The Ministry of Finance acts as the financial regulator

The MFCR is responsible for developing the financial market policy in the area of capital markets and drafting legislation governing the capital markets, as well as setting the stage for innovation-related projects. The Czech Ministry of Finance performs regular capital market analyses and ensure the Czech membership in the international financial institutions and bodies of the European Union in the capital market area (MFCR, 2022[39]).[7]

In 2019, the MFCR introduced the National Strategy for the Development of the Capital Market in the Czech Republic 2019 –23. Within the government-approved strategy, it was noted that the Czech capital markets fail to sufficiently fulfil the function of efficient allocation of unutilised savings towards enterprises who need funding and that the banking system prevails. The Strategy for market development called, among others, for more diversity in the SME financing offering with alternatives to bank financing and subsidies from the European Union, as well as greater support for innovation in finance (MFCR, 2019[19]). Regarding the regulatory approach, the Strategy stresses the need to remove unnecessary regulatory burdens and costs, except for those that draw from the requirements of EU law. In addition, regulatory stability was highlighted as important.

1.3.3. Assessing the current regulatory and supervisory frameworks as they relate to FinTech activity

"Wait and See" approach taken by the CNB

The primary regulatory framework in the Czech Republic with regard to the financial sector is set by the EU regulatory framework. With regard to innovations in finance, the Czech Republic has so far followed a "wait and see" approach when it comes to new forms of activity (e.g. crowdfunding). In the absence of an EU regulation specific to some innovative digitally enabled financial services, where existing frameworks are not applicable, the Czech Republic has in the past avoided introducing a custom national legislative framework for such services. This has often resulted in either new actors, including some FinTechs, remaining outside the regulatory perimeter, or an interpretation of existing regulatory framework to extend to the new services, requiring their providers to apply to a license already defined.

The "wait and see" approach taken by Czech policy makers might be sought to avoid fragmentation across the EU and reduce regulatory burden, in particular for innovative activities in early stages of development and at a point in time when they pose low systemic risk. However, on average, bespoke regulatory frameworks for alternative finance provide for a wider range of permitted activities than pre-existing frameworks, while they also create more explicit obligations (World Bank and CCAF, 2019[40]). Previous empirical evidence suggests that the introduction of explicit regulation appears to significantly increase retail crowdfunding volumes (Rau, 2020[41]).

The separation between underlying technology used to perform traditional financial services and completely new financial services enabled by innovative technology are becoming increasingly unclear. The introduction of the Artificial Intelligence (AI) Act proposal by the EU (European Commission, 2021[42]) may in some way be seen as an acknowledgement that complete technological neutrality may not be possible, given the fact that some technologies introduce completely new risks into the financial sector. In contrast, the use of application programming interfaces (APIs) has been leveraged by regulation to create open banking frameworks in the EU and elsewhere. Further, technological innovation now spurs outside the financial sector and is replicated or adjusted to financial services by non-financial firms such as big techs. This changes significantly the composition of financial sector actors and is a constant challenge to supervision that is entity-based.

Promoting competition is currently a secondary order objective, with possible impact on consumer interests

Neither the CNB nor the MFCR have an official mandate with regard to promoting competition in the financial sector, although the CNB considers competitiveness in the payment service providers sector as part of its mission to keep financial stability and credibility (CNB, 2023[43]). The Office for the Protection of Competition follows the legislation in Act No. 143/2001 Coll., on the Protection of Competition.[8] The office focuses on anti-competitive conduct investigations and mergers market share assessments. Competition in the financial services sector has not been at the focus of attention in the past years in the Czech Republic (ÚOHS, 2023[44]). Regarding FinTech activity, this lack of prioritisation might enable incumbents to give rise to barriers to entry of FinTechs, related for example to the reported difficulties in accessing consumers' banking data (see Section 1.2). The complementary and disruptive role of FinTechs to the activity of incumbents may not supported by Czech authorities and their supervisory compliance is mostly viewed through a micro-prudential and even risk averse perspective, rather than embracing their possible competitive advantages. Encouraging consumers to compare financial services options ("shopping" for financial services) and providers and the unbundling of products is not part of the existing financial literacy campaigns.

According to CNB officials, consumer protection issues are integrated within the work of the two supervision departments, where those departments need to balance both micro-prudential and consumer protection objectives, as well as AML/CFT requirements. Feedback from CNB officials indicate that actions in the area of consumer protection are often performed in reaction to complaints while CNB-initiated examinations do not happen often. According to the CNB, monitoring of fees and analysis of market organisational aspects such as market concentration and barriers to entry are located beyond the scope of the CNB financial supervision.

Efforts to better align the current consumer protection framework with recommended best-practices could be considered by Czech Authorities. According to the G20/OECD High-Level Principles on Financial Consumer Protection, *"there should be oversight bodies (dedicated or not) explicitly responsible for financial consumer protection, with the necessary authority to fulfil their mandates. They require clear and objectively defined responsibilities and appropriate governance; operational independence; accountability for their activities; adequate powers; resources and capabilities; defined, effective and transparent enforcement framework and clear and consistent regulatory processes"* (OECD, 2022[45]). According to other best practices with respect to consumer protection, "*operating as a stand-alone [consumer protection] department provides the benefits of independence and greater levels of resources and authority… Regardless of organisational structure, there should be a clear separation between financial consumer protection supervision and prudential supervision, or else prudential supervisory priorities will often end up dominant"* (Jaeger, Chien and Fathallah, 2014[46]).

Supervision in the area of payment services providers

The CNB has been facing elevated demand for authorisation for the various payment entities, a prominent sector among Czech FinTechs, since the implementation of PSD2 in 2018 (CNB, 2020[47]). In parallel, the CNB has been expressing dissatisfaction with the quality of application submitted and approval ratios have been quite low in the payment sector in the past several years. As regards AML/CFT compliance in the payments area, the CNB assessed that a large number of non-bank payment service providers were risky from this perspective in 2020 (CNB, 2021[48]). Since the enactment of the current Act on Payments in 2018, the number of non-bank payment service providers, both small and "large",[9] has been declining according to CNB statistics. In particular, the number of small payment service providers, which required only a registration and not a lisence prior to 2018, has sharply declined (Figure 1.8). The incidence of suspended proceedings or rejected applications in the payments sector has been higher than in other financial market sectors (OECD, 2022[1]).

The CNB has identified small payment institutions and small e-money issuers as having exploited the domestic legislative environment for their business activities, without often having at least minimum ties with the Czech market neither from an ownership nor from a clientele perspective (CNB, 2021[48]). On-site examinations identified recurring inconsistencies between the business plans submitted in the licensing proceedings and the entity's actual activities and shortcomings arising from the formal regulation of processes and activities in internal rules, which do not correspond to the actual functioning of these entities (CNB, 2021[48]).

Figure 1.8. Summary of regulated and registered payment and electronic money institutions in the Czech Republic

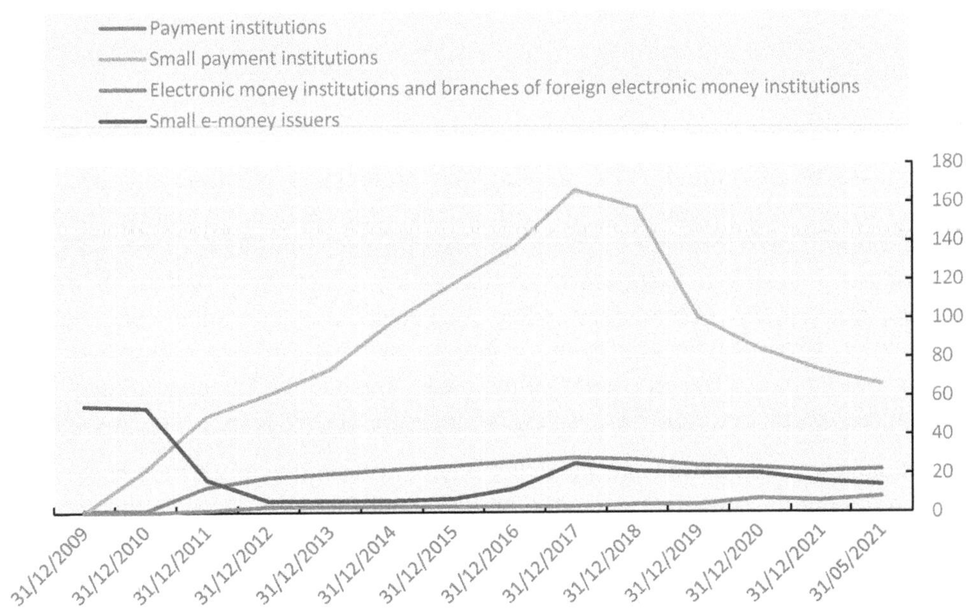

Source: Based on data from CNB (2022[49]), Regulated institutions and registered financial market entities lists, https://apl.cnb.cz/apljerrsdad/JERRS.WEB07.INTRO_PAGE?p_lang=en.

Timelines for licence approvals for payment institutions and for small payment institutions were the longest compared with other types of licenses issued by the CNB, 25 and 18.3 months on average, respectively, in 2021. For comparison, average length of proceedings completed in 2021 for credit institutions and non-bank consumer lenders was 13.1 and 14.1 months respectively. In addition, the application rate for these types of licences, and small-scale payment institutions' licences in particular, has been high in recent years.

Cultural differences between CNB and FinTechs could partially explain lack of co-operation

The culture of an organisation might be an elusive concept to define, let alone to quantify. Regulatory rules do not involve the determination of the culture of firms. The dominant culture among financial regulators and supervisors in the Czech Republic resulted from past financial events and is prescribed by the legal objectives of each organisation. The CNB's objective in the area of supervision, as defined by law, is to ensure financial stability and the safe and sound operation of the financial system in the Czech Republic, contributing to achieving its primary objective – price stability. The main components of the functional organisation of supervision are prudential supervision, conduct of business supervision and also AML/CFT supervision. The choice of a particular organisational structure of financial supervision entails trade-offs and no one structure is considered superior. Despite benefits of an integrated supervision, in this respect, prudential and conduct of business supervision require different approaches and cultures and a single institution might not be able to have the flexibility to effectively encompass both (Llewellyn, 2006[50]). Clear autonomy and independence of the consumer protection department within an integrated regulator/supervisor could alleviate such tensions at least in the on-going supervision of entities.

Cultural differences between the CNB and FinTechs might partially explain some difficulty in the co-operation by both sides revolving around the licensing and supervision in the payment service providers' sector discussed earlier. Results of the OECD (2022[1]) questionnaire focused on Czech FinTechs show that lack of regulatory clarity, obtaining a license from the CNB and red tape are the highest-ranked challenges to FinTechs development.

1.4. OECD questionnaire findings

In June 2022, the OECD (2022[1]) launched an online open questionnaire on FinTech activity in the Czech Republic. As of 25 August 2022, 22 FinTech companies provided detailed responses to this questionnaire, out of a total universe of c.100 Czech FinTech companies. These companies are headquartered in the Czech Republic or in the Slovak Republic, and 42% of these FinTechs target only the Czech market. In terms of geography of operations, more than half have headquarters in the Czech Republic, but equally, half of responding FinTechs have operations on a pan-European level through passporting rights.[10] The possibility of foreign non-EU FinTech companies benefitting from a relatively lower regulatory burden and of prey firms establishing in the Czech market is a possible concern to Czech authorities, given potential risks to customer safety and investor protection (OECD, 2022[1]).

Furthermore, most respondent firms operate in the payments and electronic money services provision and the majority of respondent firms are in the seed stage of their lifecycle. Firms in the seed and early stages usually are the ones that benefit the most from the collaboration and interaction with industry mentors and government officials (World Bank, 2022[51]), to navigate regulatory requirements and to learn from veteran experiences.

1.4.1. Data accessibility is core for FinTechs and mostly accessed through APIs

Access to data is critical for FinTechs and data is at the core of most FinTech activity (e.g. artificial intelligence business models in trading; lending; blockchain-based finance (OECD, 2021[52]). FinTechs are technology-native and combine the agility of start-ups with data processing and crunching abilities. Indeed, more than 60% of respondents to the OECD questionnaire stated that access to both financial and non-financial data is beneficial to their business development (Figure 1.9). The OECD survey shows that most innovations used by respondent Czech FinTechs evolve around data, data sharing and data usage for the development of products and services. Ninety-one percent of firms use API innovation, more than half of respondent firms use big data and 68% of firms use cloud computing – all evolving around data at the core of their business model (Figure 1.9).

Figure 1.9. Czech FinTech perceptions on data availability and types of innovation used

In number of firms responding to the 2022 OECD Questionnaire

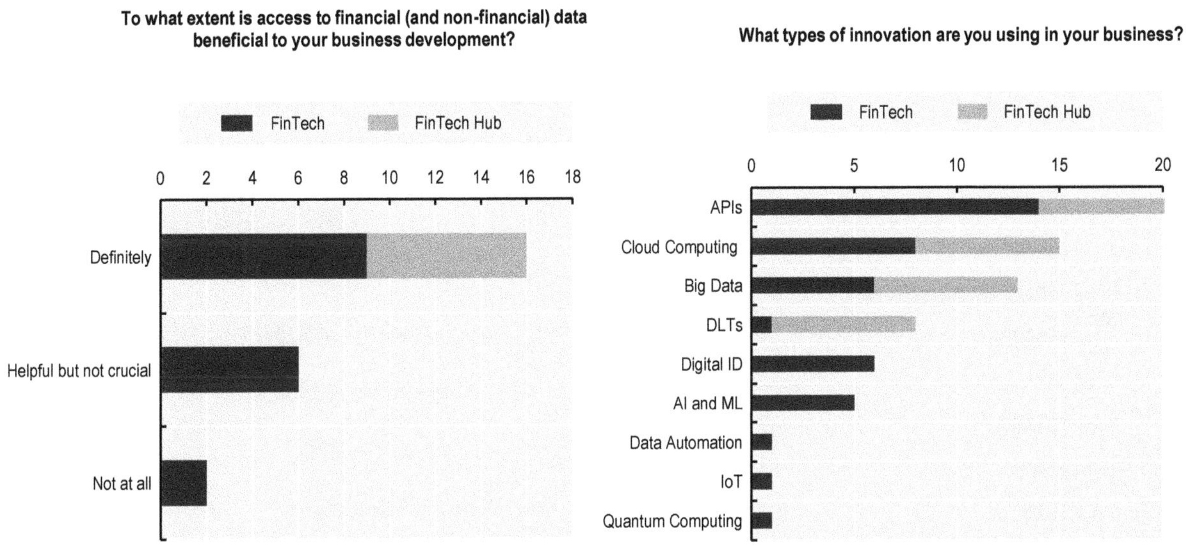

Note: The FinTech Hub is an association that aims to increase the level of innovation and competitiveness of the digital market in the Czech Republic and Central Europe. This category includes seven responses from FinTechs operating under their aegis.
Source: OECD (2022[1]), The FinTech Ecosystem in the Czech Republic, https://doi.org/10.1787/068ba90e-en.

Given the key role data plays in FinTech innovation, unequal access to data and potential dominance in the sourcing of big data by few large players could reduce the capacity of smaller players to compete in the market for Fintech innovation-based products and services (OECD, 2021[52]). To that end, greater availability of data can be conducive to the development of start-up companies with possible beneficial impact on competitive conditions in financial markets.

Incumbent financial firms usually have costly legacy and potentially obsolete infrastructure and rather inefficient processes associated to such infrastructure, which, combined with cultural reluctance for change may prevent or slow down in-house FinTech innovation. As FinTechs operate with third-party data, interdependences are created with data and digital service providers that might pose new risks to the system, such as the concentration on new dominant unregulated players. The accelerated adoption of digital technologies and FinTech products and services by customers as well as heightened demand for such products, particularly since the COVID-19 pandemic, is driving co-operation between incumbent financial institutions and FinTechs which can facilitate their access to data.

Most respondents to the questionnaire highlighted the importance of accessing financial data for their business (80%), and more than 50% highlighted the need to access personal data, which serves for the personalisation of products and services, along with non-financial data (59%), potentially spurring the financial inclusion of underbanked customers (LHS of Figure 1.10).

APIs are the most frequent form of tool allowing for data accessibility by FinTechs (86%), along with aggregators and special purchases from specialised firms (59%). Screen scraping (own data production) is also a frequent form of data gathering, used by 55% of respondents to the questionnaire (RHS of Figure 1.10).

When it comes to FinTechs sharing their own data, 77% of respondents reported that they do not share data beyond what is required by law, for different reasons. For larger firms, data is part of their key inputs; for early-stage firms, data is not part of their monetisation case yet.

Figure 1.10. Czech FinTech reported data needs

In number of firms responding to the 2022 OECD Questionnaire

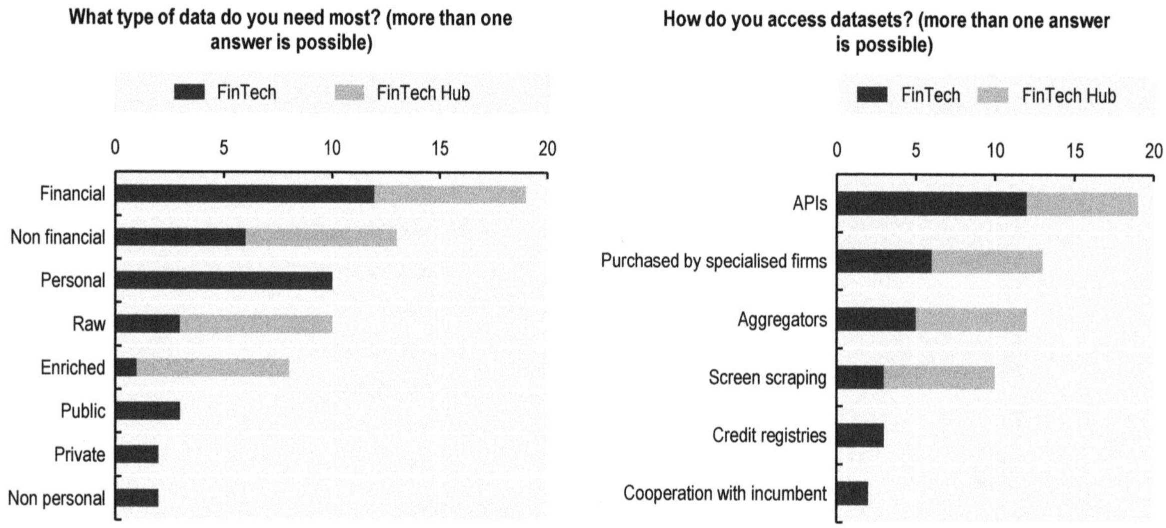

Note: The FinTech Hub is an association that aims to increase the level of innovation and competitiveness of the digital market in the Czech Republic and Central Europe. This category includes seven responses from FinTechs operating under their aegis.
Source: OECD (2022[1]), The FinTech Ecosystem in the Czech Republic, https://doi.org/10.1787/068ba90e-en .

Even when it comes to data sharing secured by formal regulatory arrangements and frameworks such as PSD2, data accessibility is not guaranteed. More than 45% of firms responding to the OECD Questionnaire have had problems accessing customer data from financial intermediaries. There are technical and strategic reasons explaining the problems: respondents reported that external APIs do not function properly in many cases, while others claimed that banks should be required by law to digitally sign documents.

There is a role for competition authorities to reduce barriers to market entry by limiting abusive dominant practices that impede competition and create risks of market concentration with detrimental impact on financial consumers, as well as systemic risk. At a minimum, existing frameworks for data sharing arrangements should be promoted and their correct implementation safeguarded.

1.4.2. Reported hurdles to FinTech innovation primarily in regulation

Financial regulation existing across the board for financial services safeguards market integrity, consumer protection and promotes financial stability (OECD, 2022[53]). From the industry standpoint, it provides for legal certainty that allows companies with innovative business models to develop and grow. At the same time, regulatory compliance is usually perceived by young start-up firms as a hurdle, given the associated cost and time commitment (World Bank, 2022[]; OECD, 2020[21]) although it is unanimously agreed that regulation is essential to keep customers safe and to preserve the stability of the system. According to the findings of the OECD questionnaire, the most important reported hurdles to FinTech innovations in the Czech Republic are related to regulation: lack of regulatory clarity (68%), red tape (64%), licensing and supervisory requirements (64%), followed by entry barriers (55% of respondents) (Figure 1.11) (World Bank, 2020[]). According to the OECD 2020 Czech Survey, resolving commercial disputes ("enforcing contracts") takes longer than on average in the OECD, and is more costly to businesses (OECD, 2020[21]).

For 11% of the respondents, finding a retaining talent seems to be a concern, and could be related to the fact that these companies employ innovative technologies and mechanisms that require specialised skillsets by highly skilled employees. Nevertheless, when it comes to digitalisation skills, the Czech Republic is clustered in the group of OECD countries characterised by the highest skills proficiency (Citibank, 2022[]). In 2020, the European Commission suggested in its country report that although the Czech Authorities are committed to the development and integration of new digital technologies, such effort is hampered by persistently low skills levels. For example, the Czech Republic still lags behind frontier Member States in terms of research and patent activities in this area (European Commission, 2020[]).

Access to funding is one of the most commonly impediments to entrepreneurship across many OECD and developing economies (OECD, 2015[]) and a reported challenge to Czech FinTech development (Figure 1.11). Overall, SMEs financing gaps may stem from an overreliance on the bank credit intermediation channel, which may be constraint particularly in times of stress. Lack of awareness about alternative funding sources and a reluctance of founders and entrepreneurs to relinquish ownership in exchange for equity financing are additional challenges. When it comes to market debt financing, SMEs have substantial structural disadvantages in obtaining such financing compared to large corporates given deal sizes and related economics of small transactions and disproportionate costs associated with such issuances (Nassr and Wehinger, 2015[]). The European Commission has also recommended support towards SMEs by making greater use of financial instruments to ensure liquidity support, reducing the administrative burden, and ensuring access to finance for innovative firms (European Commission, 2020[]).

There may be a need to clarify processes for regulatory processes such as licensing and authorisation and/or to educate new market entrants around applicable regulatory frameworks, particularly in areas of FinTech innovation, to address some of the reported impediments to FinTech development. It could also be noted that, interestingly, most Czech FinTechs operate in non-regulated sectors; the perceived burden of regulation evidenced by the OECD questionnaire could perhaps further incentivise FinTechs to develop activity in non-regulated sectors to avoid such burden. The complex administrative procedure of establishment was also identified as one of the main obstacles for start-ups in the Czech Republic by the European Commission (European Commission, 2022[]). The Commission therefore recommended that Czech Authorities remove the barriers hampering the development of a fully functioning innovation ecosystem (European Commission, 2019[]).

An additional challenge signalled by FinTech respondents is the issues of access to market and business development (OECD, 2022[1]). Regulatory sandboxes are one of the policy tools used to assist companies in overcoming the challenges on market access, as by creating an open dialogue between the regulator and the firm, they provide agility to the supervisory and regulatory framework (World Bank, 2020[61]; 2020[62]). Indeed, regulatory sandboxes are beneficial to both parties: they allow innovators to test on a small scale their products, services and delivery mechanisms (as evidenced by the United Kingdom experience), while providing the regulator with intelligence on developments, trends and emerging risks (Bromberg, Godwin and Ramsay, 2017[]; World Bank, 2020[]; Kalifa, 2021[]; World Bank, 2020[]).

Figure 1.11. Czech FinTech challenges

In number of firms responding to the 2022 OECD Questionnaire

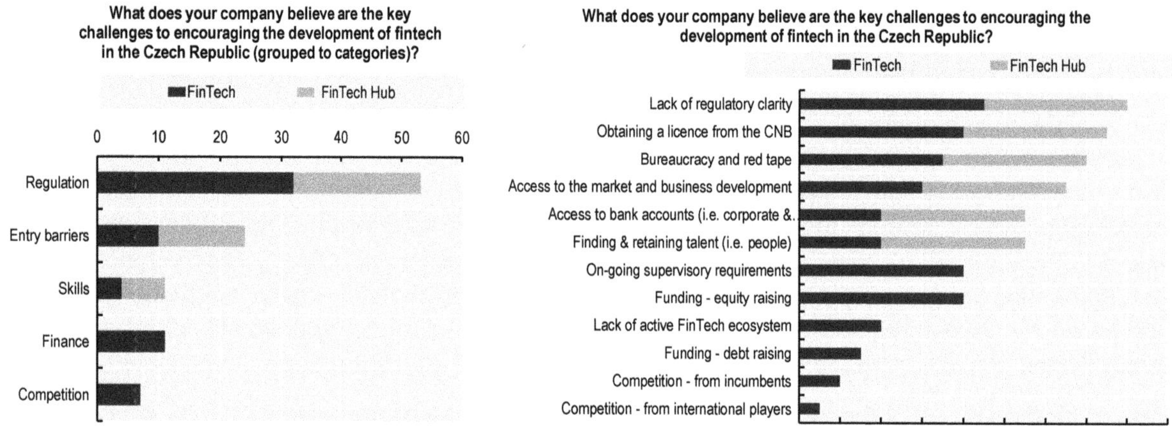

Note: More than one answer is possible. The FinTech Hub is an association that aims to increase the level of innovation and competitiveness of the digital market in the Czech Republic and Central Europe. This category includes seven responses from FinTechs operating under their aegis.
Source: OECD (2022[1]), The FinTech Ecosystem in the Czech Republic, https://doi.org/10.1787/068ba90e-en.

1.4.3. Czech FinTechs are heavily dependent on personal resources for funding

Access to finance constitutes one of the challenges for FinTech companies in the Czech Republic (see Section 1.2). Based on the responses to the OECD Questionnaire, the main investment source for Czech FinTechs is personal resources (37% of respondents), which is consistent with start-up and SME companies deploying own funds and friends and family financing (Berger and Udell, 2003[]). Czech entrepreneurs rely mainly on their own resources and seed capital (68% of companies secured seed capital from own sources while only 48% were able to find an investor in a recent industry survey (Deloitte Česká Republika, 2022[]). 14% of start-ups raised initial funding from family or relatives and friends, while 5% took a loan from a bank.

Domestic VC funding appears to be the second most important funding source in the group of respondents (18%). When combined with international VCs, this source of funding becomes the most widely used in the group (33% combined VC). These responses reflect the increase in VC activity by domestic funds in the Czech Republic although there is still room to develop VC funding further in the country relative to the levels observed in the rest of Europe (see Section 1.2). Czech FinTechs are also looking for VC as their main investment source in the future (Figure 1.12).

It should be also noted that none of the FinTech firms responding to the OECD Questionnaire received funding from the public sector (local or national) (Figure 1.12).

Most respondents have a neutral or favourable opinion of the Czech Republic as an easy place to raise investment (OECD, 2022[1]). A caution note can be made on this assertion, as only FinTechs who have successfully raised funding for their innovation have answered the OECD Questionnaire, so there is a possible survival bias and sample selection bias in this exercise (Keogh and Johnson, 2021[]).

Figure 1.12. Czech FinTech access to finance, 2022

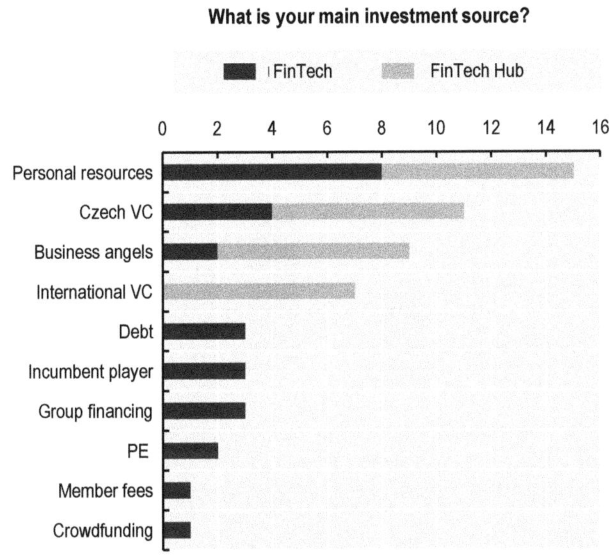

Note: The FinTech Hub is an association that aims to increase the level of innovation and competitiveness of the digital market in the Czech Republic and Central Europe. This category includes seven responses from FinTechs operating under their aegis.
Source: OECD (2022[1]), The FinTech Ecosystem in the Czech Republic, https://doi.org/10.1787/068ba90e-en.

Another interesting observation of the responses to the OECD Questionnaire relates to the exit strategy of responding FinTechs: the majority of FinTechs report to be in the business to be acquired by incumbents or larger FinTechs/BigTechs (M&A accounting for more than 64% of the responses). Although this is understandable, it is not conducive to increased competition in the market for financial services and are subject to the terms of the acquisitions (OECD, 2022[1]).

1.4.4. Czech FinTechs are interested in a regulatory sandbox

More than 77% of respondents to the OECD Questionnaire believe that it would be beneficial to introduce a regulatory sandbox in the Czech Republic. According to the OECD survey, 73% of respondent FinTechs would be interested in a sandbox with a focus on data if it were to become available (Figure 1.13). Two-thirds of these would only be interested depending on the terms of such a sandbox. This highlights the importance of a well-thought design and structure of any future sandbox arrangement. It also highlights a possible lack of clear understanding of what a sandbox involves from the FinTech side, underscoring the importance of clear communication and a required educational effort that may need to be undertaken in such effort.

Sandbox arrangements enable firms to test innovative financial products and services and develop business models that are based on the use of innovative technologies and mechanisms, subject to the specific rules applied by the competent supervisory authorities. Although sandboxes can involve the use of legally provided discretions by supervisory authorities, the baseline assumption for regulatory sandboxes is that firms are required to comply with all relevant rules applicable to the activity they are undertaking (BIS, 2018[]). In addition, sandboxes do not entail the disapplication of regulatory requirements that must be applied because of EU law (ESMA, EBA and EIOPA, 2019[]).

Figure 1.13. Perceived interest in a regulatory or data sandbox

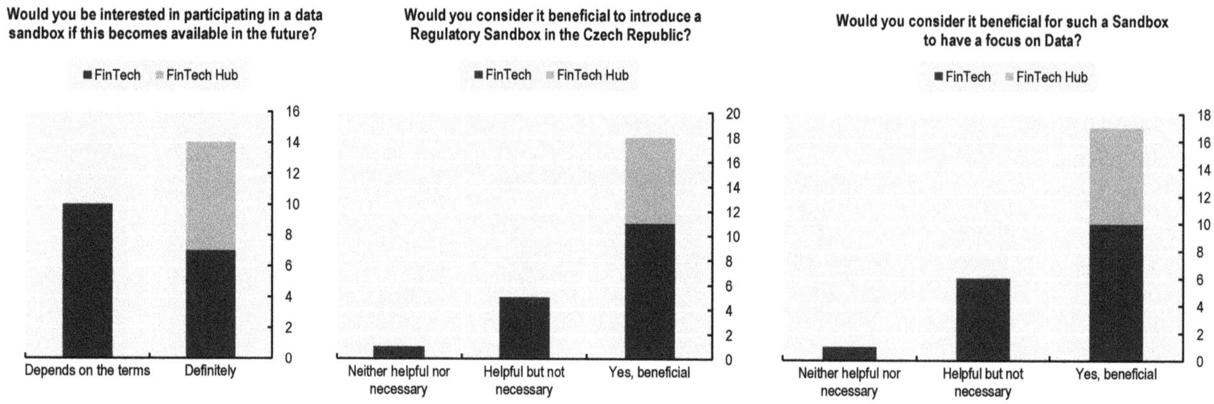

Note: The FinTech Hub is an association that aims to increase the level of innovation and competitiveness of the digital market in the Czech Republic and Central Europe. This category includes seven responses from FinTechs operating under their aegis.
Source: OECD (2022[11]), The FinTech Ecosystem in the Czech Republic, https://doi.org/10.1787/068ba90e-en.

Regulatory sandboxes can foster innovation in the financial sector while allowing supervisors to observe and address emerging risks of the deployment of innovative technologies in finance, with benefits that extend to all stakeholders involved. They allow supervisors to enhance their understanding of innovative mechanisms deployed by FinTechs that may alter the risk profile of certain financial activities, which, in turn, may have a beneficial impact on the development of adequate policy responses to such innovations. Importantly, they reduce regulatory uncertainty for FinTechs and can help lower the perceived regulatory burden that has been observed in the OECD survey of FinTechs in the Czech Republic. In terms of funding, empirical evidence suggests a beneficial impact of sandbox participation for fundraising of companies, facilitating access to finance which has been highlighted as one of the most important impediments to the establishment and growth of SMEs in the Czech Republic and beyond (Cornelli et al., 2020[]). Sandboxes can also promote competition, and allow the development of new products and services, diversifying financial consumer offering and possibly promoting financial inclusion or other policy objectives, such as sustainability (FCA, 2022[])

When it comes to a data sandbox, this could conceptually involve a controlled environment on which FinTechs could test innovations based on data sharing, data usage and business models that rely heavily on data, without a regulatory component in the sandbox. For example, the development, testing and validation of artificial intelligence-based products and of machine-learning-based models could be envisaged in a controlled environment of a data sandbox, or the development of distributed ledger technology-based activity for the recording and analysis of large volumes of (unstructured) data. Indicatively, such data sandbox could provide real and synthetic datasets available through the sandbox or collected through API calls or could consist of an effort to collectively gather such datasets in co-operation with participating firms and depending on their needs.

1.5. Opportunities for policy makers to address challenges and close gaps with best practices

To observe the legal mandates of supervisors – i.e. market integrity, ensure financial stability, protect consumers – and at the same time unleash the potential of data in financial services and stimulate innovation in the financial sector, it is crucial to look at key characteristics and best practices in the fields of FinTech policies and data in finance.

FinTech companies have the potential to boost economic growth, create skilled jobs, and leverage the power of data for the benefit of clients. Thanks to data portability rules in the context of open banking, FinTech-developed products allow customers to benefit from cheaper or more personalised services and change financial services providers with more ease. FinTechs are widely seen as crucial facilitators for more effective and competitive financial markets, as well as for extending access to credit for people who have historically been underserved (OECD, 2022[27]).

There are indications that the current dialogue between the CNB and FinTechs may not be optimal and would benefit from an improved setting for constructive dialogue and exchange of information that would benefit both sides. FinTechs report regulatory requirements and supervisory actions as prominent hurdles to their operations, while at the same time, CNB officials are showing dissatisfaction with license applications, as well as lack of preparedness. This brings rise to opportunities for policy makers to address the main hurdles found in the FinTech ecosystem. With the best practices in mind, the current Czech practices are analysed and possible gaps and challenges are noted. The identified gaps form the basis of the recommendation for considering the implementation an innovation facilitator in the form of a regulatory sandbox as one of the ways to alleviate some of the most important gaps and challenges for FinTech development in the Czech Republic.

1.5.1. Regulatory sandboxes as a tool to optimise communication between Authorities and FinTechs

While the CNB shows dissatisfaction with FinTech license applications and holds a 'wait and see' approach for regulation/supervision of new forms of activity, FinTechs perceive regulatory and supervisory issues are the main hurdles to their development, citing regulatory unclarity as a main issue. This results in multiple rounds of formalised exchanges between the two sides during license application processes, contributing to a longer authorisation process. As FinTechs are often small enterprises that do not enjoy deep financial pockets as their incumbent counterparts, speed to market is imperative and the slowing of this speed could compromise their financial viability.

Customised guidance, which can take the form of greater transparency and clear guidance to prepare for the submission of an application for license, would benefit individual FinTechs and Authorities alike. While FinTechs could as a result make more informed decisions, identify potential opportunities, develop tailored strategies, and ensure compliance with applicable regulations, regulators could better monitor the activities of FinTechs and ensure compliance with the applicable regulatory framework without the bending of any rules. The current CNB FinTech contact point, although perfectly adequate in terms of quality, may be insufficient in terms of capacity and perhaps unable to cover forthcoming likely increasing demand for guidance by FinTechs, considering new of upcoming regulations in the EU space (Markets in Crypto-assets (MiCA) Regulation, Distributed ledger technology (DLT) pilot regime, Artificial Intelligence (AI) Act proposal).

A form of innovation facilitator could be a way to promote the diffusion of understanding and knowledge of regulations, supervision and norms, while at the same time informing the regulatory/supervisory authorities of the impacts of regulations, thus not only driving innovation in the market, but also within the regulatory/supervisory bodies. While continuing to apply current rules and regulations, innovation facilitators can enhance legal certainty without bending the rules for FinTechs.

Two main categories of innovation facilitators are identified in the European Union according to the European Supervisory Authorities (ESA's) Joint Report on Regulatory Sandboxes and Innovation Hubs (ESMA, EBA and EIOPA, 2019[]):

- Innovation hubs: these provide a dedicated point of contact for firms to raise enquiries with competent authorities on FinTech-related issues and to seek non-binding guidance on the conformity of innovative financial products, financial services or business models with licensing or registration requirements and regulatory and supervisory expectations.

- Regulatory sandboxes: these provide a scheme to enable firms to test, pursuant to a specific testing plan agreed and monitored by a dedicated function of the competent authority, innovative financial products, financial services or business models. Sandboxes may also imply the use of legally provided discretions by the relevant supervisor (with use depending on the relevant applicable EU and national law) but sandboxes do not entail the disapplication of regulatory requirements that must be applied because of EU law.

General analysis of strengths, weaknesses, opportunities and threats

The potential benefits of innovation facilitators are widely acknowledged by OECD members. Regulatory sandboxes are a suitable approach to address fast technological development in the European market. A recent study of the European Commission states that they are essential in areas such as FinTech, to prevent pre-mature market exclusion for emerging business models that do not comply with existing regulatory frameworks without giving these models an opportunity to prove that they can offer adequate levels of protection of users (European Commission, 2019▯).

Possible weakness of the facilitator might arise from an inadequately chosen design. This means either a design that does not provide sufficiently appealing functionalities addressing FinTech needs; or a design that does not fit the characteristics of the local FinTech – and broader financial services – market environment. For this reason, an extensive analysis is required before any specific design characteristics are recommended to ensure the feasibility of the recommended design.

Regulatory sandboxes can provide the opportunity for advancing regulation through proactive regulatory learning, enabling regulators to gain better regulatory knowledge and to find the best means to regulate innovations based on real-world evidence (European Union, 2020▯).

At the same time, regulatory sandboxes need to respect and should foster the application of the principles of subsidiarity and of proportionality, as well as of the precautionary principle (European Union, 2020▯). Proper framework for governance and accountability of the innovation facilitator is vital to enable the regulator to evaluate internally the performance and achievements of the innovation facilitator as well as for the purposes of accountability (European Parliament, 2020▯).

Viability evaluation

The benefits of innovation facilitators to markets can be seen by multiple such initiatives taken over several years of experience across both the European Union as well as globally. Several OECD economies have opted for the regulatory sandbox approach to regulate FinTech while enhancing an innovative ecosystem and preserving the stability of the financial sector. Regulatory sandboxes have come to be associated with FinTech innovation (World Bank, 2020▯). A regulatory sandbox might provide an open dialogue environment to assess motivations, business models and common understanding of FinTech activities and regulatory measures (ESMA, EBA and EIOPA, 2019▯). The jurisdiction historically driving the development is the United Kingdom, where the first ever sandbox was implemented in 2016. Another leading example in FinTech innovation regulation is Singapore, where the Monetary Authority of Singapore (MAS) policy intent was based on a balanced approach in promoting financial development and ensuring a safe and sound financial sector, and in sync with its objective to harness technology and to improve the efficiency of the financial markets (Fan, 2018▯). In advanced economies, the Central Bank, the Financial Supervisory Authority or the Securities Regulator oversees regulatory sandboxes (see Table 1.1).

Table 1.1. Sandbox arrangements across OECD and non-OECD economies

Country	Type of Regulator	Year of implementation
United Kingdom	Financial Supervisor	2016
Australia	Securities Regulator	2016
Singapore	Central Bank	2016
Canada	Securities Regulator	2017
Japan	Financial Supervisor, Other Govt. Body	2017
Netherlands	Central Bank, Financial Supervisor	2017
Lithuania	Central Bank	2018
Norway	Ministry of Finance	2018
Switzerland	Financial Supervisor, Other Govt. Body	2018
Taiwan	Financial Supervisor	2018
Denmark	Financial Supervisory Authority	2019
South Korea	Securities Regulator, Financial Supervisor	2019
Austria	Financial Market Authority	2019
Denmark	Financial Supervisory Authority	2019
Spain	Bank of Spain	2020
Hungary	Central Bank	2020
Poland	Financial Supervisory Authority and Ministry of Finance	2020
Greece	Central Bank	2021
Italy	Central Bank, Securities Regulator, Insurance Supervisor and Ministry of Finance and Economy	2021
Latvia	Financial Markets Authority	2021
Slovak Republic	Central Bank	2022

Source: Presentation delivered at the OECD Workshop in Prague on 24 November 2022.

To ensure efficient functioning of the innovation facilitator and usefulness for the local Czech market, the design should consider both local needs as well as best practices taken from existing initiatives to support financial innovation. Equal access opportunities to innovation facilitators and transparent eligibility criteria are essential to ensure a level playing field. Clear and transparent objectives need to be combined with sufficient resources and tools to create an environment for the envisioned knowledge transfer and viable functioning of the innovation facilitator.

The detailed recommendations provided thereafter on the optimal design of an innovation facilitator and the substantive arguments backing such recommendations provide the necessary but not sufficient conditions for the undertaking of this project by the Czech Authorities. Institutional buy-in and political willingness to consider the establishment of a regulatory sandbox by Czech Authorities is a prerequisite for the success of such an endeavour. The necessary internal set-up for such a facilitator to be effective, including organisational independence and a clear mandate from the relevant authorities are additional parameters to promote the successful implementation of such endeavour. The lack of deployment of necessary resources, both in scale and in skill, for the establishment of an innovation facilitator at the organisational and operational level would be a major risk to the implementation of this recommendation. The identified barriers to FinTech growth provided earlier in the process, combined with the current feasibility analysis, provide for evidence-based arguments for the need of such facilitator in the Czech Republic as one of the ways to alleviate constraints to FinTech development in the Czech Republic. The recommendations provided thereafter are taking into consideration the feasibility of such endeavour in the context of the Czech financial markets environment, FinTech ecosystem, regulatory and supervisory environment and European-level developments in the financial innovation space.

Expected impact of a regulatory or a data sandbox in the Czech Republic

The European Commission's Digital Finance Strategy in Chapter 4.1 highlights that "Firms should be able to rely on close co-operation between national supervisory innovation facilitators within the European Forum of Innovation Facilitators (EFIF), and a new EU digital finance platform." (European Commission, 2020[]). That puts Czech innovative companies in a possibly disadvantaged position. Although the Fintech contact point of the Czech National Bank participates in the meetings of the EFIF, it is a contact point with limited scope, giving Czech innovators limited options compared to their competitors from other EU member states, particularly when it comes to cross-border collaboration of European regulatory sandboxes.

A Czech regulatory sandbox could bring benefits to regulators, innovators and consumers and ensure that Czech FinTechs do not lose their competitiveness. It could directly address the need for better dialogue between the supervisor and the Czech FinTechs and would cover for the possibly limited capacity of the current contact point in a future environment of growing needs by FinTechs considering new or forthcoming EU regulatory frameworks, or current shifts in the financial services market. The facilitator will allow the supervisor to gain traction with innovative business models that can be tested in the facilitator to inform their supervisory activity. This may mean identifying potential risks and hazards to the sector and providing better data and technology to support financial regulators and supervisors. Importantly, it may reduce regulatory uncertainty for FinTechs and may help lower the perceived regulatory burden for FinTechs in the Czech Republic that has been observed in the OECD consultation (OECD, 2022[1]).

The establishment of an innovation facilitator, such as a regulatory sandbox, can foster innovation in the financial sector while allowing supervisors to observe and address emerging risks of the deployment of innovative technologies in finance, with potential benefits that extend to all stakeholders involved. They may allow supervisors to enhance their understanding of innovative mechanisms deployed by FinTechs that may alter the risk profile of certain financial activities, which, in turn, may have a beneficial impact on the development of adequate policy responses to such innovations.

Financial facilitators in the form of data sandboxes could provide enhanced data-sharing capabilities, building a platform for companies to test data-based business models or innovative ideas based on real or synthetic data accessible in a controlled environment. A data sandbox could conceptually involve a controlled environment on which FinTechs would use specifically prepared data to test business models or innovative ideas that rely heavily on data, without a regulatory component. Indicatively, such data sandboxes could provide tailor-made real and synthetic datasets available to sandbox participants, provided data can be gathered from public authorities and/or market participants.

References

Advokátní deník (2022), "Crowdfunding se nově zařadí mezi běžné investiční nástroje", https://advokatnidenik.cz/2022/04/28/nova-zakonna-regulace-zaradi-crowdfunding-mezi-bezne-investicni-nastroje/ (accessed on 4 August 2022). [7]

Berger, A. and G. Udell (2003), *Small Business and Debt Finance*, Springer-Verlag, https://doi.org/10.1007/0-387-24519-7_13. [66]

BIS (2018), "Implications of fintech developments for banks and bank supervisors", *Basel Committee on Banking Supervision, Sound Practices*, http://www.bis.org (accessed on 29 August 2022). [69]

Bromberg, L., A. Godwin and I. Ramsay (2017), "Fintech sandboxes: Achieving a balance between regulation and innovation", *Journal of Banking and Finance Law and Practice*, Vol. 28/4, pp. 314-336. [63]

CCAF (2021), *The 2nd Global Alternative Finance Market Benchmarking Report*, CCAF, https://www.jbs.cam.ac.uk/faculty-research/centres/alternative-finance/publications/the-2nd-global-alternative-finance-market-benchmarking-report/ (accessed on 25 January 2022). [6]

Citibank (2022), *Digital Money Index*, https://www.citibank.com/icg/sa/digital_symposium/digital_money_index/ (accessed on 29 August 2022). [55]

CNB (2023), *Regulace a dohled nad platebními institucemi a institucemi elektronických peněz - Česká národní banka*, https://www.cnb.cz/cs/dohled-financni-trh/vykon-dohledu/postaveni-dohledu/regulace-a-dohled-nad-platebnimi-institucemi-a-institucemi-elektronickych-penez/ (accessed on 20 January 2023). [43]

CNB (2022), *ARAD - Time Serie System - Czech National bank*, https://www.cnb.cz/cnb/STAT.ARADY_PKG.STROM_DRILL?p_strid=0&p_lang=EN (accessed on 4 August 2022). [18]

CNB (2022), *CNB launches FinTech contact point - Czech National Bank*, https://www.cnb.cz/en/cnb-news/press-releases/CNB-launches-FinTech-contact-point (accessed on 20 June 2022). [38]

CNB (2022), *Financial market supervision - Czech National Bank*, https://www.cnb.cz/en/supervision-financial-market/ (accessed on 16 June 2022). [36]

CNB (2022), *Long-term supervisory strategy of the Czech National Bank - Czech National Bank*, https://www.cnb.cz/en/supervision-financial-market/long-term-supervisory-strategy-of-the-czech-national-bank/ (accessed on 24 June 2022). [37]

CNB (2022), *Regulated institutions and registered financial market entities lists*, https://apl.cnb.cz/apljerrsdad/JERRS.WEB07.INTRO_PAGE?p_lang=en (accessed on 17 June 2022). [49]

CNB (2021), *Financial Market Supervision Report 2020*, https://www.cnb.cz/export/sites/cnb/en/supervision-financial-market/.galleries/aggregate_information_financial_sector/financial_market_supervision_reports/download/fms_2020.pdf (accessed on 22 June 2022). [48]

CNB (2020), *Financial Market Supervision Report 2019*, https://www.cnb.cz/export/sites/cnb/en/supervision-financial-market/.galleries/aggregate_information_financial_sector/financial_market_supervision_reports/download/fms_2019.pdf (accessed on 22 June 2022). [47]

Cornelli, G. et al. (2020), "Inside the regulatory sandbox: effects on fintech funding", BIS, https://www.bis.org/publ/work901.htm (accessed on 29 August 2022). [71]

Czech Statistical Office (2022), *Information Society in Figures 2022 Czechia and EU*, http://www.plzen.czso.cz (accessed on 9 November 2022). [17]

Czech Statistical Office (2022), *Innovation activities of enterprises - 2018 to 2020 | CZSO (in Czech)*, https://www.czso.cz/csu/czso/inovacni-aktivity-podniku-20182020 (accessed on 9 November 2022). [15]

Deloitte Česká Republika (2022), *Jak se v Česku daří startupům*, https://www2.deloitte.com/cz/cs/pages/press/articles/jak-se-v-cesku-dari-startupum.html (accessed on 29 August 2022). [67]

EBA (2022), *Opinion of the European Banking Authority on its technical advice on the review of Directive (EU) 2015/2366 on payment services in the internal market (PSD2)*. [30]

Ecommerce Europe and EuroCommerce (2022), *European E-Commerce report 2022*, http://www.ecommerce-europe.eu (accessed on 20 January 2023). [9]

ESMA, EBA and EIOPA (2019), *FinTech: Regulatory sandboxes and innovation hubs*, https://ec.europa.eu/info/publications/180308-action-plan-fintech_en. (accessed on 5 May 2023). [70]

European Commission (2022), *Consultation document - Targeted consultation on open finance framework and data sharing in the financial sector*, EUROPEAN COMMISSION DIRECTORATE-GENERAL FOR FINANCIAL STABILITY, FINANCIAL SERVICES AND CAPITAL MARKETS UNION, https://ec.europa.eu/info/sites/default/files/business_economy_euro/banking_and_finance/documents/2022-open-finance-consultation-document_en.pdf (accessed on 10 May 2022). [34]

European Commission (2022), *Country Report-Czechia Accompanying the document Recommendation for a COUNCIL RECOMMENDATION on the 2022 National Reform Programme of Czechia and delivering a Council opinion on the 2022 Convergence Programme of Czechia*, https://eur-lex.europa.eu/legal-content/EN/ALL/?uri=CELEX%3A52022SC0605 (accessed on 29 August 2022). [59]

European Commission (2022), *European Innovation Scoreboard - Country Profile - Czechia*, https://ec.europa.eu/assets/rtd/eis/2022/ec_rtd_eis-country-profile-cz.pdf (accessed on 9 November 2022). [11]

European Commission (2022), *European Innovation Scoreboard 2022 and Regional Innovation Scoreboard 2021*, https://ec.europa.eu/research-and-innovation/en/statistics/performance-indicators/european-innovation-scoreboard/eis (accessed on 9 November 2022). [14]

European Commission (2022), *Proposal for a REGULATION OF THE EUROPEAN PARLIAMENT AND OF THE COUNCIL on harmonised rules on fair access to and use of data (Data Act)*, https://eur-lex.europa.eu/legal-content/EN/TXT/?uri=COM%3A2022%3A68%3AFIN (accessed on 3 August 2022). [33]

European Commission (2022), *REGULATION (EU) 2022/868 OF THE EUROPEAN PARLIAMENT AND OF THE COUNCIL of 30 May 2022 on European data governance and amending Regulation (EU) 2018/1724 (Data Governance Act)*, https://eur-lex.europa.eu/legal-content/EN/TXT/?uri=CELEX%3A32022R0868 (accessed on 3 August 2022). [32]

European Commission (2021), *Data and surveys - SAFE*, https://single-market-economy.ec.europa.eu/access-finance/data-and-surveys-safe_en (accessed on 4 November 2022). [22]

European Commission (2021), *Proposal for a REGULATION OF THE EUROPEAN PARLIAMENT AND OF THE COUNCIL LAYING DOWN HARMONISED RULES ON ARTIFICIAL INTELLIGENCE (ARTIFICIAL INTELLIGENCE ACT) AND AMENDING CERTAIN UNION LEGISLATIVE ACTS*, https://eur-lex.europa.eu/legal-content/EN/TXT/?uri=CELEX%3A52021PC0206 (accessed on 3 August 2022). [42]

European Commission (2020), *COMMUNICATION FROM THE COMMISSION TO THE EUROPEAN PARLIAMENT, THE COUNCIL, THE EUROPEAN ECONOMIC AND SOCIAL COMMITTEE AND THE COMMITTEE OF THE REGIONS A European strategy for data*, https://eur-lex.europa.eu/legal-content/EN/TXT/?uri=CELEX%3A52020DC0066 (accessed on 3 August 2022). [31]

European Commission (2020), *Digital finance package*, https://ec.europa.eu/info/publications/200924-digital-finance-proposals_en (accessed on 1 August 2022). [35]

European Commission (2020), *Digital Finance Strategy for the EU*, https://eur-lex.europa.eu/legal-content/EN/TXT/?uri=CELEX:52020DC0591 (accessed on 23 January 2023). [77]

European Commission (2020), *Recommendation for a COUNCIL RECOMMENDATION on the 2020 National Reform Programme of Czechia and delivering a Council opinion on the 2020 Convergence Programme of Czechia*, https://eur-lex.europa.eu/legal-content/EN/TXT/?qid=1591720698631&uri=CELEX%3A52020DC0503 (accessed on 22 August 2022). [56]

European Commission (2019), *2019 SBA Fact Sheet Czechia*, https://ec.europa.eu/docsroom/documents/38662/attachments/7/translations/en/renditions/native (accessed on 24 January 2023). [26]

European Commission (2019), *Recommendation for a COUNCIL RECOMMENDATION on the 2019 National Reform Programme of the Czech Republic and delivering a Council opinion on the 2019 Convergence Programme of the Czech Republic*, https://www.vlada.cz/assets/evropske-zalezitosti/aktualne/Doporuceni-pro-CR-pro-rok-2019-schvalena-Radou-ECOFIN_1.pdf (accessed on 5 September 2022). [60]

European Commission (2019), *Study supporting the interim evaluation of the innovation principle - Publications Office of the EU*, https://op.europa.eu/en/web/eu-law-and-publications/publication-detail/-/publication/e361ec68-09b4-11ea-8c1f-01aa75ed71a1 (accessed on 23 January 2023). [73]

European Parliament (2020), *Regulatory sandboxes and innovation hubs for FinTech - Publications Office of the EU*, https://op.europa.eu/en/publication-detail/-/publication/f7485a21-084d-11eb-a511-01aa75ed71a1/language-en/format-PDF/source-279143019 (accessed on 23 January 2023). [75]

European Union (2020), *Council Conclusions on Regulatory Sandboxes and Experimentation Clauses as tools for an innovation-friendly, future-proof and resilient regulatory framework that masters disruptive challenges in the digital age*, https://eur-lex.europa.eu/legal-content/EN/TXT/?uri=CELEX%3A52020XG1223%2801%29 (accessed on 5 August 2022). [74]

Fan, P. (2018), "Singapore Approach to Develop and Regulate FinTech", *Handbook of Blockchain, Digital Finance, and Inclusion, Volume 1: Cryptocurrency, FinTech, InsurTech, and Regulation*, pp. 347-357, https://doi.org/10.1016/B978-0-12-810441-5.00015-4. [76]

FCA (2022), *Supporting innovation in ESG data and disclosures: the digital sandbox sustainability pilot*, https://www.fca.org.uk/publication/corporate/digital-sandbox-sustainability-pilot-report.pdf (accessed on 22 August 2022). [72]

FinTech Cowboys (2022), *Fintechová mapa České republiky - jaro 2022: přes 100 fintechů*, https://fintechcowboys.cz/fintechova-mapa-ceske-republiky-jaro-2022-pres-100-fintechu/ (accessed on 4 August 2022). [3]

ICLG (2021), *Fintech Law and Regulations, Czech Republic 2021-2022*, https://iclg.com/practice-areas/fintech-laws-and-regulations/czech-republic (accessed on 17 June 2022). [2]

Jaeger, J., J. Chien and S. Fathallah (2014), *Establishing a Financial Consumer Protection Supervision Department*, World Bank, https://openknowledge.worldbank.org/handle/10986/25894 (accessed on 9 December 2022). [46]

Kalifa, R. (2021), "Kalifa Review of UK FinTech", https://www.gov.uk/government/publications/the-kalifa-review-of-uk-fintech. [65]

Keogh, D. and D. Johnson (2021), "Survival of the funded: Econometric analysis of startup longevity and success", *Journal of Entrepreneurship, Management and Innovation*, Vol. 17/4, pp. 29-49, https://doi.org/10.7341/20211742. [68]

Llewellyn, D. (2006), "Institutional structure of financial regulation and supervision: the basic issues", *World Bank seminar, Aligning Supervisory Structures with Country Needs, Washington DC*, https://paulmaharg.com/letr/references/storage/M2HKVKHB/Llewellyn%20-%202005%20-%20Institutional%20structure%20of%20financial%20regulation%20an.pdf (accessed on 19 December 2022). [50]

Lukas Valusek and Lenka Kučerová (2022), *Restructuring and insolvency law in the Czech Republic*, CMS, https://cms.law/en/int/expert-guides/cms-expert-guide-to-restructuring-and-insolvency-law/czech-republic (accessed on 15 December 2022). [25]

Mcgowan, M. and D. Andrews (2018), "Design of insolvency regimes across countries", *Economics Department Working Papers*, No. 1504, OECD, http://www.oecd.org/eco/workingpapers. (accessed on 15 December 2022). [24]

McKinsey (2022), *Europe's fintech opportunity*, https://www.mckinsey.com/industries/financial-services/our-insights/europes-fintech-opportunity (accessed on 4 May 2023). [4]

MFCR (2022), *Basic Information | Capital Market | Ministry of Finance of the Czech Republic*, https://www.mfcr.cz/en/themes/capital-market/basic-information (accessed on 1 July 2022). [39]

MFCR (2020), *Financial Literacy Measurement Results 2020: ATTITUDES TO FINANCE AND BEHAVIOR ON THE FINANCIAL MARKET*, https://financnigramotnost.mfcr.cz/cs/pro-odborniky/mereni-urovne-financni-gramotnosti/2020/postoje-k-financim-a-chovani-3272/ (accessed on 4 August 2022). [20]

MFCR (2019), *National Strategy for the Development of the Capital Market in the Czech Republic for the period of 2019-2023*, https://www.mfcr.cz/assets/en/media/201903-National-Strategy-CZ-Capital-Market.pdf (accessed on 1 July 2022). [19]

MFCR (2017), *Act No 370/2017 Sb. on Payments*, https://www.mfcr.cz/assets/cs/media/Zak_2017-370_Zakon-o-platebnim-styku-anglicky-preklad-k-1-4-2019.pdf (accessed on 24 August 2022). [29]

MFCR and EU (2022), *Home | Capital guide*, https://www.kapitalovypruvodce.cz/en/ (accessed on 5 August 2022). [28]

Nassr, I. and G. Wehinger (2015), "Unlocking SME finance through market-based debt: Securitisation, private placements and bonds", *OECD Journal: Financial Market Trends* , Vol. 2014/2, https://www.oecd.org/finance/Unlocking-SME-finance-through-market-based-debt.pdf (accessed on 22 August 2022). [58]

OECD (2022), *Business innovation statistics and indicators*, https://www.oecd.org/sti/inno-stats.htm#indicators (accessed on 9 November 2022). [10]

OECD (2022), "Marketplace and FinTech lending for SMEs in the COVID-19 crisis", *OECD Business and Finance Policy Papers*, No. 02, OECD Publishing, Paris, https://doi.org/10.1787/ff11697f-en. [27]

OECD (2022), *OECD Science, Technology and Innovation Scoreboard*, https://www.oecd.org/sti/scoreboard.htm#publications (accessed on 9 November 2022). [16]

OECD (2022), *Recommendation of the Council on High-Level Principles on Financial Consumer Protection*, https://legalinstruments.oecd.org/en/instruments/OECD-LEGAL-0394 (accessed on 16 December 2022). [45]

OECD (2022), *The FinTech Ecosystem in the Czech Republic*, OECD Publishing, Paris, https://doi.org/10.1787/068ba90e-en. [1]

OECD (2022), *Why Decentralised Finance (DeFi) Matters and the Policy Implications - OECD*, https://www.oecd.org/finance/why-decentralised-finance-defi-matters-and-the-policy-implications.htm (accessed on 18 March 2022). [53]

OECD (2021), *Artificial Intelligence, Machine Learning and Big Data in Finance Opportunities, Challenges and Implications for Policy Makers*, https://www.oecd.org/finance/artificial-intelligence-machine-learningbig-data-in-finance.htm. (accessed on 22 August 2022). [52]

OECD (2020), *Innovation Diffusion in The Czech Republic a Regional Approach*. [13]

OECD (2020), *OECD Economic Surveys: Czech Republic 2020*, OECD Publishing, Paris, https://doi.org/10.1787/1b180a5a-en. [21]

OECD (2015), *Opportunities and Constraints of Market-Based Financing for SMEs OECD Report to G20 Finance Ministers and Central Bank Governors*, https://doi.org/10.1787/fmt-2014-5js3bg1g53ln. [57]

OECD/Eurostat (2018), *Oslo Manual 2018: Guidelines for Collecting, Reporting and Using Data on Innovation, 4th Edition*, The Measurement of Scientific, Technological and Innovation Activities, OECD Publishing, Paris/Eurostat, Luxembourg, https://doi.org/10.1787/9789264304604-en. [78]

Prague Stock Exchange (2022), *Consolidated Annual Report 2021*, https://www.pse.cz/userfiles/annual_reports/49eb1d3c5e38da03d4deb5dd9aac3df2.pdf (accessed on 4 November 2022). [79]

R&D&I Council (2019), *Innovation Strategy of the Czech Republic 2019 - 2030 | Research and development in Czech republic*, https://www.vyzkum.cz/FrontClanek.aspx?idsekce=867922 (accessed on 8 November 2022). [12]

Rau, P. (2020), "Law, Trust, and the Development of Crowdfunding", *SSRN Electronic Journal*, University of Cambridge, https://doi.org/10.2139/SSRN.2989056. [41]

Startups, G., Atomico and dealroom.co (2021), *Coming of age: Central and Eastern European startups*. [23]

ÚOHS (2023), *Office for the Protection of Competition | Annual reports*, https://www.uohs.cz/en/information-centre/annual-reports.html (accessed on 24 January 2023). [44]

ÚOHS (2023), *Office for the Protection of Competition | History of the Office*, https://www.uohs.cz/en/about-the-office/history-of-the-office.html (accessed on 24 January 2023). [80]

Visa (2022), *Contactless Payments Around the Globe*, https://www.visa.com.bs/visa-everywhere/innovation/contactless-payments-around-the-globe.html (accessed on 31 October 2022). [5]

World Bank (2022), *Regulation and Supervision of Fintech: Considerations for EMDE Policymakers*, https://openknowledge.worldbank.org/handle/10986/37345 (accessed on 23 August 2022). [51]

World Bank (2021), *The Global Findex Database 2021*, https://www.worldbank.org/en/publication/globalfindex (accessed on 4 November 2022). [8]

World Bank (2020), *Doing Business 2020*, https://doi.org/10.1596/978-1-4648-1440-2. [54]

World Bank (2020), "Global Experiences from Regulatory Sandboxes", *Fintech Note*, No. 8, World Bank, Washington DC, https://doi.org/10.1596/34789. [62]

World Bank (ed.) (2020), *How Regulators Respond To FinTech*, World Bank, Washington, DC, https://doi.org/10.1596/33698. [64]

World Bank (2020), "How Regulators Respond To FinTech : Evaluating the Different Approaches – Sandboxes and Beyond", *Fintech Note*, No. 4, https://doi.org/10.1596/33698. [61]

World Bank and CCAF (2019), *Regulating Alternative Finance: Results from a Global Regulator Survey.*, World Bank and CCAF, https://www.jbs.cam.ac.uk/faculty-research/centres/alternative-finance/publications/regulating-alternative-finance/ (accessed on 20 April 2022). [40]

Notes

[1] All funds raised via an online digital marketplace, including P2P/marketplace lending (debt-crowdfunding), balance sheet lending, equity-crowdfunding and non-investment crowdfunding.

[2]According to the Oslo Manual, product innovation is a new or improved good or service that differs significantly from the firm's previous goods or services and that has been introduced in the market (OECD/Eurostat, 2018▯).

[3] The PSE currently operates three venues in which companies' shares are offered and traded. These are primarily the STANDARD and PRIME markets, while there is also the smaller START market intended for SMEs. The START trading venue launched in 2018 is dedicated to smaller, innovative companies. Its market capitalisation reached CZK 8 590 million at the end of 2021, attracting nine issues during the year (Prague Stock Exchange, 2022▯).

[4] The Act on Payments [Act No. 370/2017 Coll.] is the national legislation from 2017 implementing the PSD2 directive.

[5] The shareholders are Air Bank, Česká spořitelna, ČSOB, Fio banka, Komerční banka, mBank, Moneta Money Bank, Raiffeisenbank and UniCredit Bank.

[6] In accordance with Act No. 6/1993 Coll., on the CNB.

[7] The mandate of the Ministry of Finance of the Czech Republic in the area of capital market regulation is laid out by Section 4 (1) of Act no. 2/1969 Coll., on the Establishment of Ministries and Other Central Government Authorities of the Czech Republic.

[8] The Office is a central administrative body independent in its decision-making practice. The Office is headed by a Chairman appointed by the President of the Czech Republic on the proposal of the Government (ÚOHS, 2023▯).

[9] with EU passportable licences.

[10] Passporting rights are one of the foundational basis of the EU single market for financial services, and enable FinTech firms (as any other financial services firms) that are authorised in any EU or EEA state to freely trade in the Czech Republic (as in any other member state) following notification of the host authorities.

2 Recommendations for a sandbox in the Czech Republic

This chapter presents recommendations on the optimal design of a feasible innovation facilitator in the Czech Republic. The proposed design caters to the specificities of the Czech Republic as identified in the analysis, including the structure of the Czech financial sector, the Czech FinTech ecosystem, the national and EU regulatory and supervisory framework and future expected developments in the regulation of financial innovation. The recommendations have been developed in close consultation with the Czech and European Authorities and draw on past experiences of sandbox models in jurisdictions where these have been established (in OECD and non-OECD member countries with a focus on European Union countries).

The design recommendations (see Executive summary for an outline) cover the definition of 'innovation' or 'innovative financial product' that would merit its inclusion; eligibility criteria for the entrepreneurs to be admitted to participate in the sandbox, including the licensing procedure; authorisation model; limits of the testing environment; exit procedures; measurements of performance; and recommended timelines. The chapter also describes regulatory and supervisory principles and/or standards, including the risk register and risk management considerations, and offers a communication strategy to ensure all stakeholders are aware of the regulatory sandbox's purpose and function. The latter is particularly important given observed misconceptions in the Czech Republic around the definition and purpose of regulatory sandboxes.

The recommended design for a Czech regulatory sandbox is based on the feasibility study for its implementation in the Czech Republic and is tailored to the specificities of the Czech ecosystem, considering relevant opportunities and limitations of the domestic environment. The key design recommendations for the Czech Regulatory Sandbox are as follows.

Definition of "innovative financial product": a new or improved financial product, service, or business strategy that leverages novel/emerging technologies to provide innovative/enhanced financial services.

Objectives of the proposed regulatory sandbox for FinTechs: facilitate innovation and speed up productive innovation; promote competition and financial inclusion in the financial sector; facilitate the adoption of new technologies; and attract FinTechs.

Recommended scope: cross-sectoral with no restrictions concerning the sector of activity, if it falls under the remit of the financial authorities, directly or indirectly. In this context, 'indirectly' refers to financial activity that may not fall under the existing definitions of activities requiring a license from Authorities but may still have an impact on the financial sector. Applicants must comply with the eligibility criteria in all cases.

Limits of the testing environment: The recommended structure advises against the provision of any waivers, restricted authorisations or other relaxation of existing applicable rules, which would anyway be against EU rules. It is recommended that a proportional application of existing regulatory and supervisory requirements, as embedded in EU financial services regulation, is used as appropriate, and at the discretion of the supervisor for firms participating in the Czech regulatory sandbox. Such proportionality can apply to the governance process and system and control requirements, board composition; financial soundness; reputation; management experience and track record. Proportionality should be applied on a case-by-case basis by the supervisor, depending on the business model and the applicable rules.

Regulatory and supervisory oversight: The recommendation for the Czech regulatory sandbox to maximise operational benefits and improve the dissemination of regulatory clarity on the one hand, and understanding of business models by the supervisor on the other hand, is to have the sandbox set up by the Authorities. The practice in all EU regulatory sandboxes has been for regulatory sandboxes to be established at the supervisory authority. Since the suggested testing framework will not offer exemptions to participating firms in the sandbox beyond those provided by national and European law, there is therefore no need for legislative changes for the establishment of a regulatory sandbox. The Czech Authorities could establish the regulatory sandbox by an internal act or by designating which posts will be dedicated to co-ordinating its operation within the relevant Authorities.

Standard regulatory vs. data sandbox: The recommendation for the Czech sandbox is to commence with the establishment of the 'standard' regulatory sandbox and, to the extent feasible, provide data-sharing when the conditions allow it. The feasibility of this option will be based on (i) the availability of datasets and ability to make these available; (ii) the capacity of the authorities participating in the regulatory sandbox. It could also be envisaged that a data sandbox without a regulatory component to it could be outsourced and/or be established outside the Czech Authorities, although even in this case the Authorities would need to participate inter alia by means of providing data. The two types of sandboxes, regulatory and data, are not mutually exclusive.

Types of data in the data sandbox: The recommendation about the Czech data sandbox will depend on the feasibility analysis of such endeavour, which, in turn, will depend to a large extent on the datasets that can be made available, taking under consideration legal and technical limitations with respect to companies participating in such facilitator, while it will also depend on the allocation of capacity to operate such a sandbox, both in terms of numbers and in terms of technical skillsets, to allow for its operation.

Synthetic data in the data sandbox: It is recommended to avoid this option at the first stages of development of the data sandbox, unless there is a willingness to deploy important resources, both internally / pre-existing and externally in terms of providers of specialised services that may not be available within the Czech authorities. In the future, depending on the availability of resources and the experience of the sandbox, Czech authorities can consider engaging in a more resource-intensive phase of the data sandbox, involving synthetic datasets.

Participants: Categories of firms that may participate and would find it useful include companies that already have a license but wish to test a new technology and/or business model; companies that do not have the required license within the financial legislation to provide the desired activity; companies where it is uncertain whether the activity requires a license within the financial legislation.

Eligibility criteria: It is recommended that participants in the regulatory sandbox hold the appropriate license for the regulated activity undertaken or are ready to apply for a license in order to have it before the start of the testing phase, if the supervisor deems that the activity falls within the perimeter of regulated financial activity. In case the supervisor deems that a license is not necessary, the Czech Authorities have the discretion to allow the company to perform the testing or not. This could be beneficial for both the Czech Authorities and the service provider, for example, if regulation in this area is being negotiated and co-operation is assessed as beneficial for familiarisation with this type of product.

Authorisation model: Participants are preselected by a special Advisory Board based on enclosed eligibility criteria, which provides a non-binding recommendation. This will then be validated or rejected by the Czech Authorities, and this does not apply to the CNB, as the CNB has no legal basis to issue such a decision. The Authority operating the sandbox would issue a decision regarding the selection upon considering the recommendation of the Advisory Board.

2.1. Definitions and objectives

2.1.1. Objectives of a regulatory sandbox

A regulatory sandbox is a framework that allows FinTech companies to test innovative new products, services, and business models in a controlled environment under the oversight of a regulatory authority and without the bending of rules. The recommended main objectives of the proposed regulatory sandbox for FinTechs in the Czech Republic are shown in Figure 2.1.

Figure 2.1. Objectives of a regulatory sandbox

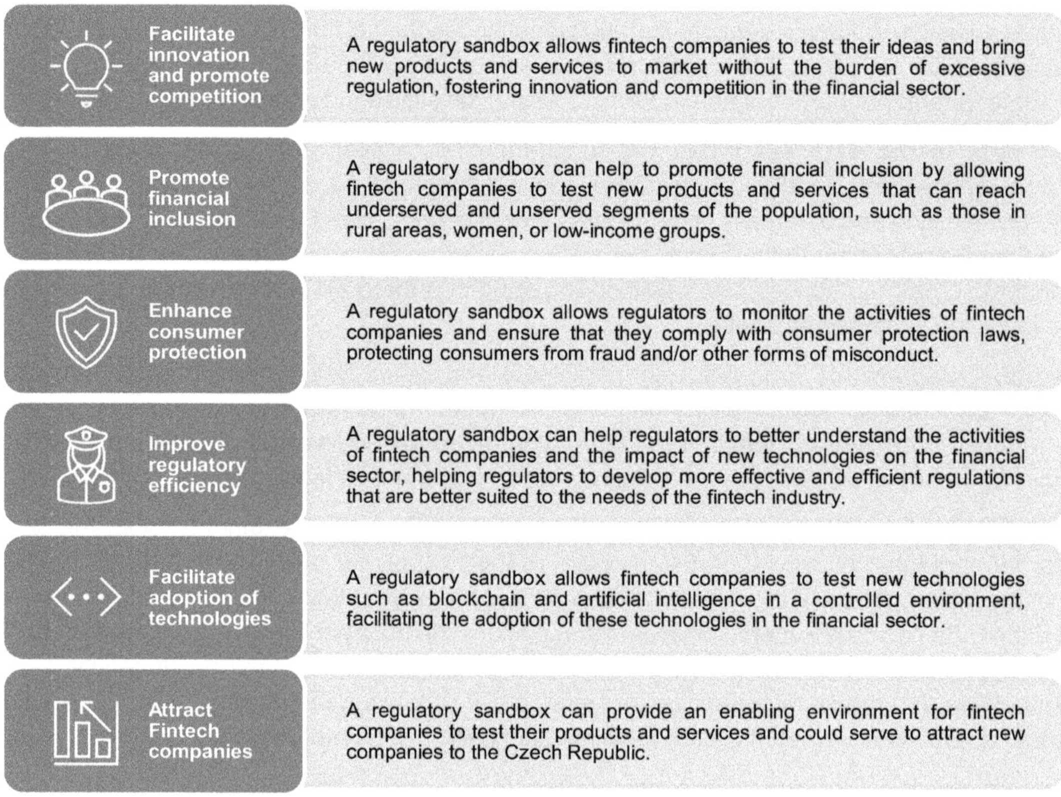

2.1.2. Understanding the concept of innovation

When creating a regulatory sandbox for FinTechs, the definition of what constitutes an innovative financial product is an important factor to consider. The definition must be precise, well-defined, and consider the rules and legislation of the Czech Republic. The regulatory sandbox can help the development and testing of new and emerging technologies while also guaranteeing that consumer protection and regulatory monitoring are maintained.

The definition of financial innovation should be comprehensive and take into account various factors. It is important to note that none of these criteria should be given preferential treatment, as they are all complementary and equally important for defining financial innovation. The first criterion is the impact of the innovation on the market and competition. Financial innovations may involve new products, services, or procedures that disrupt established market structures or create new market opportunities. The second criterion is the effect of the innovation on customer convenience and choice. Financial innovations may include new products, services, or procedures that expand customer options or improve user experience. The third criterion is the influence of the innovation on financial stability and risk management. Financial innovations can involve new products, services, or procedures that enhance the efficiency and resilience of the financial system or reduce systemic risks (Figure 2.2). The three criterions should be viewed as complementary, having similar importance.

Figure 2.2. Understanding the concept of innovation

Additionally, as the FinTech sector and regulatory landscape develop over time, the definition of an innovative financial product may also change. Therefore, it is important to take a holistic approach rather than merely focusing on the technology used, keeping in mind that innovation can also emerge from new business models or new ways of delivering financial services (OECD/Eurostat, 2018[1]).

In the case of the Czech regulatory sandbox, it is recommended that the definition of the term "innovative financial product" should refer to a new or improved financial product, service, or business strategy that leverages novel or emerging technologies to provide innovative and enhanced financial services. Payment service providers, aggregators, crypto-asset related firms, distributed ledger technology-based financial activity, robo-advisory platforms, and peer-to-peer lending platforms are a few examples of possible products in this category. A product, service, or business model that makes use of current technology in new or creative ways will also be referred to as an innovative financial product. For example, fraud can be detected using artificial intelligence, and credit risk can be evaluated using big data analytics.

2.1.3. Distinction between sandbox types

'Standard' regulatory sandbox

'Standard' regulatory sandboxes are types of innovation facilitators schemes that enable firms to test, pursuant to a specific testing plan agreed and monitored by a dedicated function of the competent authority, innovative financial products, financial services or business models (ESMA, EBA and EIOPA, 2019[2]). Table 2.1 displays a list of operational and planned regulatory sandbox within the EU.

Table 2.1. List of operational and planned regulatory sandboxes in the EU

#	Country	Sandbox	Banking	Insurance	Securities	Website
EU						
1	AT	✓	✓	✓	✓	https://www.fma.gv.at/en/fintech-point-of-contact-sandbox/fma-sandbox/
2	BE	N				
3	BG	Announced				https://www.minfin.bg/en/news/10967
4	CY	N				
5	CZ	N				
6	DE	N				
7	DK	✓	✓	✓	✓	https://www.dfsa.dk/Supervision/Fintech/FT-lab
8	EE	Planned	✓	✓	✓	https://www.ebrd.com/news/2019/moving-the-regulatory-debate-

#	Country	Sandbox	Banking	Insurance	Securities	Website
						forward-ebrd-and-estonia-are-working-on-their-first-sandbox.html
9	EL	Planned	✓	✓	✓	https://www.bankofgreece.gr/en/main-tasks/supervision/regulatory-sandbox
10	ES	Planned			✓	https://portal.mineco.gob.es/RecursosNoticia/mineco/prensa/noticias/2022/20220627-PR_AI_Sandbox_EN.pdf
11	FI	N				
12	FR	N				
13	HR	N				
14	HU	✓	✓	✓	✓	https://www.mnb.hu/en/innovation-hub/regulatory-sandbox
15	IE	N				
16	IT	✓	✓	✓	✓	https://www.dt.mef.gov.it/it/dipartimento/consultazioni_pubbliche/consultazione_regolamento.html
17	LT	✓	✓	✓	✓	
18	LU	N				
19	LV	✓	✓	✓	✓	https://www.bank.lv/en/co-operation/support-for-fintech-and-innovations/regulatory-sandbox
20	MT	✓	✓	✓	✓	https://www.mfsa.mt/fintech/regulatory-sandbox/
21	NL	✓	✓	✓	✓	https://www.dnb.nl/en/sector-information/supervision-stages/prior-to-supervision/innovationhub-and-regulatory-sandbox/
22	PL	Planned	✓	✓	✓	https://www.knf.gov.pl/?articleId=69563&p_id=18
23	PT	Planned	✓	✓	✓	http://dre.pt/application/conteudo/132133788
24	RO	N				
25	SE	N				
26	SK	✓	✓	✓	✓	https://nbs.sk/en/financial-market-supervision1/fintech/regulatory-sandbox/
27	SL	N				
EFTA						
28	IS	N				
29	LI	N				
30	NO	✓	✓	✓	✓	https://www.finanstilsynet.no/en/topics/fintech-and-regulatory-sandbox/finanstilsynets-regulatory-sandbox/
31	CH	✓	✓	✓	✓	https://www.finma.ch/en/news/2019March 20190315-mm-fintech/
32	UK	✓	✓	✓	✓	https://www.fca.org.uk/firms/innovation/regulatory-sandbox

Source: Based on ESMA, EBA and EIOPA (2019[2]), FinTech: Regulatory sandboxes and innovation hubs, https://ec.europa.eu/info/publications/180308-action-plan-fintech_en, and publicly available information on the websites mentioned in the table.

A regulatory sandbox may offer several key benefits to both FinTech companies and regulatory authorities in the Czech Republic. Regulatory sandboxes allow companies to test and validate their products and services in a real-world environment, gaining valuable insights into their feasibility and viability. This can help to reduce the risk of failure for new innovations. Additionally, regulatory sandboxes provide regulatory authorities with an opportunity to assess the potential impact of these innovations on consumers and the wider economy, allowing them to make informed decisions about the regulation of these products and services.

The scope of a regulatory sandbox can be extended to include data-sharing functionalities. There is often confusion between the concepts of data sharing and a data sandbox. Data sharing refers to the practice of sharing data between organisations or entities for a specific purpose, such as improving customer experience or fraud detection. On the other hand, a data sandbox is a secure testing environment that allows organisations to experiment with data without risking sensitive information or breaching data privacy regulations. Both concepts involve the sharing of data, either between different parties or within a controlled environment, for the purpose of testing or analysis. Both data sharing and a data sandbox can also potentially lead to innovation and the development of new products or services, as well as improvements in efficiency and cost savings. Additionally, both concepts can raise concerns around data privacy and security and require careful consideration of legal and regulatory frameworks. However, there are some differences in their purpose, scope, data ownership and security measures (Figure 2.3).

Figure 2.3. Data sharing vs. data sandbox

	Data Sharing	Data Sandbox
Purpose	Done to exchange data between different organisations or individuals for specific purposes, such as improving business operations or research outcomes.	Specifically designed to allow experimentation and innovation with data.
Scope	Typically involves sharing data between known and trusted parties, and the scope is limited to the specific data sets and purposes agreed upon.	Open to a wider range of participants, and the scope can be more flexible, allowing for more experimentation.
Data Ownership	In data sharing environments, the ownership and control of the data remains with the original owner, and they may place restrictions on how the data can be used or shared.	Ownership and control of data can be shared among participants, and the data sandbox can provide a neutral space for participants to collaborate on new ways to use the data.
Privacy, Security	Privacy protection levels should be the same in any of the two options. Data-sets created within data sandboxes are proprietary in nature as they tend to constitute intellectual property of participants building these (e.g. synthetic datasets) and participants are therefore usually required to sign non-disclosure agreements for the participation in such data sandboxes.	

The recommendation for the Czech regulatory sandbox is to consider the establishment of a 'standard' regulatory sandbox and only extend its scope by incorporating data-sharing capabilities when the conditions allow it. Enriching the standard regulatory sandbox with a data-sharing option could be envisaged based on (i) the availability of datasets and ability to make these available; (ii) the capacity of the authorities participating in the regulatory sandbox.

It could also be envisaged that a data sandbox without a regulatory component could be outsourced and/or exist outside the Authorities, although even in this alternative the Czech Authorities would likely need to participate *inter alia* by means of providing data.

Data sandbox

Data sandboxes are testing environments where companies can experiment with new data-driven products and services or components of products/services that are based on data in a similar setting. In a data sandbox, companies have the freedom to test new product elements using real-world data or synthetic data, in a controlled environment.

Companies could build data-driven models that would form part of a business model or service and which may not necessarily directly involve financial market activity. Indicatively, one example of a potential use case for a data sandbox would be a FinTech lender wishing to create and validate a machine learning-based model for the assessment of creditworthiness of potential borrowers. Any datasets of SME financial data (e.g. debt metrics including debt repayment history; amount of debt; credit mix; debt capacity; metrics related to collateral pledged, traditional credit scores) made available to the FinTech in the context of such data sandbox, combined with other non-traditional data, would allow the FinTech to create, calibrate and validate new models for alternative credit scoring.

Such a data sandbox could offer several key benefits to FinTech companies in the Czech Republic. The data sandbox would help to foster innovation by providing companies with access to real-world data, or synthetic data mimicking the real world, allowing them to test, train and validate new products and technologies. Often, FinTechs have a problem getting access to valuable data sets, even though their products depend on data, because this data is privately held by financial institutions or by the public sector, and it might be a cost barrier to the FinTechs or straightforward impossible to access it. Depending on the data provided, it should be assessed who will be able to access the data and under what legal and technological commitments. In theory, for public data, no restrictions should apply. Indeed, some authorities already make large amount of public data available with different options of access including data download and API access (see Table 2.2 for example). For synthetic data, sensitivities other than privacy, which are resolved through the generating process, may remain. The FCA and the Bank of Spain have not made access to their synthetic data available outside of the sandbox (see further below).

In addition, a data sandbox may offer participant various technological tools to facilitate access to data, data manipulation and analysis and the creation of additional features of the data.

The concept of a data sandbox has gained traction globally as a way for regulators to allow experimentation with new financial technologies, while also managing any associated risks. The goal of these data sandboxes is to create a supportive environment for innovation and growth in the financial sector, while also ensuring the protection of consumers and maintaining the stability of the financial system. Some possible data types that could be shared and accessed in a data sandbox for a use by FinTechs are provided in Table 2.2 below.

The recommendation for the establishment of the 'standard' regulatory sandbox as a first step will allow the Czech Authorities to gather any datasets that may not be immediately available, or to format those that are not available in the format that would allow their usage by firms. In parallel, it would allow some time for the operational preparations within the authority (e.g. in terms of IT infrastructure requirements or appointment of external consultants in case of outsourcing). Input is required by Czech Authorities on the availability of such datasets (currently or in the near future), as a first step, and on whether these could be made available in some form (e.g. anonymised or with other deferential privacy methods, synthetic, other), to allow the assessment of feasibility of the data sandbox.

Synthetic data in a data sandbox

Synthetic data is artificially produced to replicate the statistical components of real data. As such, to generate a synthetic data, access to the real data must also be available, must also be available for some synthetic data generation techniques such as Agent-based modelling and Generative Adversarial Networks (GANs). But it does not need to be shared to other entities after the synthetic data was successfully generated. The synthetic data generation process provides an alternative to real data and can produce inexhaustible amounts of simulated data, and a potentially cheaper way of improving the predictive power and enhancing the robustness of machine learning models, especially where real data is scarce or expensive or contains personally identifiable information that cannot be shared. Importantly, synthetic data is not anonymised data as it is created for artificial entities. The generation of synthetic data requires high statistical and technological expertise.[1] To develop the synthetic data sets, the FCA collaborated with financial services industry participants, innovators, academics, technologists and data scientists. In the synthetic data pilot in Spain, the objective was to create a synthetic data set and to analyse whether it can substitute for real world data for testing purposes. Synthetic data was generated out of the original confidential data held by the national supervisor (Bank of Spain). The real data never left the premises of the supervisor, and no external user accessed the data; the supervisor remains the legal owner of the synthetic data; the generation process was done with a software provided by a private firm whose services were acquired through a tender procedure.

When it comes to the use of synthetic data in a Czech data sandbox, the recommendation is to avoid this option at the first stages of development of a sandbox, unless there is a willingness to deploy important resources, both internally / pre-existing and externally in terms of providers of specialised services that may not be available within the Czech Authorities. In the future, depending on the availability of resources and the experience of the regulatory sandbox, Czech Authorities can consider engaging in a more resource-intensive phase of a data sandbox, involving synthetic datasets.

The creation of synthetic data, that could be useful for FinTechs for testing and validating their products, requires access to a real-world data set, otherwise it cannot be built. For example, if there is no availability of micro data on loans to individuals, it is impossible to generate a synthetic dataset with similar statistical properties.[2] Moreover, to create a synthetic dataset, it is necessary to know all the distribution parameters of the actual data set, which can only be obtained by working with data specialists. In the third place, if such a synthetic dataset were to be built, it also must be trusted by the FinTechs as being statistically similar to actual data, which is a key consideration in the process. Synthetic data can also be fully compliant with data protection obligations (as compared against anonymisation and pseudonymisation where there is still a risk of trace-back of individuals). Practical examples of data sandboxes can be found in Annex C.

The recommendation for a Czech data sandbox will depend on the feasibility analysis of such an endeavour. The feasibility of a data sandbox in the Czech Republic will depend to a large extent on the datasets that can be made available, taking under consideration legal and technical limitations, to companies participating in such facilitator, while it will also depend on the allocation of capacity, both in terms of numbers and in terms of skillsets, to allow its operation. In addition, financial and other authorities might not possess the kind of data that is valuable to FinTechs. It is thus important to get a good understanding of the data needs of the Czech FinTechs through dialogue and surveys. Table 2.2 provides the types of datasets that have been made available in data or other regulatory sandboxes globally in OECD and non-OECD countries, other data sources not included in this table would also need to be considered depending on the Czech Authorities' availability. The selection of data types should be made with the needs of Czech FinTechs in mind through dialogue within the regulatory sandbox.

Table 2.2. Datasets made available to FinTechs in data or other sandboxes in OECD and non-OECD countries

Type of data	Datasets	Type	Example of established sandbox (country)
Financial Data	SME lending: loan history, credit card history, current account history, SME directors, COVID-19 lending, factoring, profit and loss, accounts receivable, lending providers.	Synthetic	FCA Digital Sandbox (UK)
	Retail and wholesale banking transactions	Synthetic	FCA Digital Sandbox (UK)
	Asset resolution dataset	Synthetic	FCA Digital Sandbox (UK)
	ESG – sustainability linked bonds	Synthetic	FCA Digital Sandbox (UK)
	Device data related to faster payments usage	Synthetic	FCA Digital Sandbox (UK)
	Annual accounts reported by non-financial firms	Synthetic	Bank of Spain synthetic data pilot (Spain)
	Loans extended to legal entities resident and non-resident and reported to the Central Credit Register	Synthetic	Bank of Spain synthetic data pilot (Spain)
	Macro financial public data – interest and exchange rates, money supply[1]	Real	Monetary Authority of Singapore website (Singapore)
	Core banking system data[2]	Test data	APIX Sandbox (AFIN[3])
	Public firms' disclosures (periodic accounts)	Real	Pilot regime in FinTech (Israel)
	Trade on the Tel Aviv Stock Exchange data	Real	Pilot regime in FinTech (Israel)
	Public administration public data[4]	Real	Open Data Platform (Colombia)

Type of data	Datasets	Type	Example of established sandbox (country)
Non-Financial Data	Planet satellite data	Synthetic	FCA Digital Sandbox (UK)
	ESG – business energy usage data	Synthetic	FCA Digital Sandbox (UK)
	ESG – cement, iron and steel production	Real	FCA Digital Sandbox (UK)
	ESG – European Red List	Real	FCA Digital Sandbox (UK)
	ESG – Sustainable Development Goal Indicators	Real	FCA Digital Sandbox (UK)
	Public administration public data[4]	Real	Open Data Platform (Colombia)

Notes:
1. The Monetary Authority of Singapore (MAS) provides Application Programming Interfaces (APIs) for developers to access relevant data from MAS and make use of the datasets for streamlining of applications and systems; the Government of Singapore (2022[3]), Monetary Authority of Singapore (MAS) APIs – Streamlining of Financial Applications through Data Singapore Government Developer Portal, https://www.developer.tech.gov.sg/products/categories/data-and-apis/mas-apis/overview.html.
2. APIX (2023[4]), Sandbox | Collaborative Integrated Development Environment (IDE).
3. AFIN is a non-for-profit entity that was jointly formed by the Monetary Authority of Singapore (MAS), the World Bank Group's International Finance Corporation (IFC) and the ASEAN Bankers Association.
4. The Ministry of Information Technologies and Communications (2023[5]), Datos Abiertos Colombia, https://www.datos.gov.co/.

2.2. Regulatory and supervisory considerations

The detailed design recommendations in the following sections relate to the regulatory sandbox recommendation, as the data sandbox option does not have a regulatory component and can be established outside the Czech Authorities at the discretion of participating parties.

2.2.1. Limits of the testing environment

The recommended structure for the Czech regulatory sandbox advises against the provision of any waivers; restricted authorisations or other relaxation of existing applicable rules, which would anyway be against EU rules. It is recommended that a proportional application of existing regulatory and supervisory requirements, as embedded in EU financial services regulation, is used as appropriate and at the discretion of the Authorities for firms participating in the Czech regulatory sandbox. Such proportionality can apply to the governance process and system and control requirements, board composition; financial soundness; reputation; management experience and track record (Deloitte, 2017[6]). Proportionality should be applied on a case-by-case basis by the Authorities, depending on the business model and the applicable rules. The addition of safeguards to protect financial consumers should be considered if there is an assessment that extraordinary risks exist or if the existing regulatory framework does not address the risks associated with the innovation being tested.

Different jurisdictions have chosen different combinations of permitted and forbidden activities for firms participating in regulatory sandboxes. The ultimate boundaries in a given testing arrangement are the result of the legal provisions and regulations applicable to financial service providers and financial products and the overall objectives pursued by authorities in establishing a testing environment. Most countries that have implemented a regulatory sandbox have not opted to set it by defining a new legal regime and the legal boundaries of the testing environment are thus dictated by the existing license regime and the discretion available to the competent supervisors in law (EBRD, 2019[7]). A greater divergence between the provisions of the testing environment and the standard regulatory licensing regime would require defining in legislation a special legal regime for the testing environment, and that might take a long time to complete and defer the implementation of a regulatory sandbox. Further it might be in contradiction with the idea of technological neutrality that supervisors pursue. Nonetheless, some jurisdictions have chosen to amend existing legislation with innovative financial service providers in mind (Australia, Switzerland), and their regimes usually include a broader set of exemption for FinTechs.

The legal options that set the regulatory and enforcement boundaries for the participants of the previously established regulatory sandboxes world-wide can be classified as one of the following:

Restricted authorisation – Partial authorisation allows to grant an authorisation to operate a regulated activity but limiting the number of customers who participate in the test, or number of products offered to the customers. The UK offers restricted authorisation for firms participating in the regulatory sandbox. The introduction of a restricted license did not require a dedicated legislation in the UK. In Switzerland, firms in the sandbox may receive or invest public funds up to CHF 1 million without obtaining a license. This exemption was introduced by the Swiss Federal Council. In parallel, a separate "Fintech license" has been introduced in the Swiss Banking Act unrelated to sandbox participation. The Fintech license provides simplifications and lower market entry requirements, as compared to the full banking license.

Proportional authorisation – Regulatory sandboxes established in EU member countries stipulate that, to the extent that participation in the regulatory sandbox involves the carrying out of a regulated activity, the appropriate license is required to be held. Any divergence between the requirements of a regular licensing application and that of an application submitted by a regulatory sandbox participant are related to the interpretation of the competent supervisor of the idea of proportionality, exerted by the supervisor's discretion. What this means in effect, is that the same proportionality is applicable to submission for a license by a non-sandbox firm. Embedded in EU financial services measures are tools to enable the proportionate application of regulatory and supervisory requirements. The joint report of the European Supervisory Authorities (ESA) points to the governance process and system and control requirements as appropriate for proportionality consideration. For the purpose of a concrete example, ESA mentions that governance system is subject to proportionality in Banking and Insurance EU laws (ESMA, EBA and EIOPA, 2019[2]).

In complement to certain supervisory relief, limitations or restrictions may be imposed for risk mitigation. Imposing limitations or other restrictions can be regarded as a lever for proportionality in the licensing or supervision process. In practice, in implementing proportionality for innovative firms, trying to lower boundaries that do not necessarily serve the purpose of the rule, EU member countries have focused on activities where the legal regime is set in national legislation, while much narrower discretionary space is taken in relation to EU laws. the Netherlands, Lithuania and Austria have stated that their respective regulatory sandboxes do not represent a new legal regime nor a "stripped down license". Rather, supervisory requirements may be adapted on a case-by-case manner within the scope of the principle of proportionality for supervision, depending on the business model, where the laws permit this. In Lithuania, the regulatory sandbox regime is governed by a resolution of the Bank of Lithuania. In Austria the establishment and operation of the regulatory sandbox was achieved by means of legislative amendment in the underlying legal framework of the Financial Market Authority (FMA). According to Austrian officials, the need to set the operation of the regulatory sandbox in a designated law had two rationales – the first was to assure that additional resources are granted to the FMA for the operation of the regulatory sandbox; the second was for the law to protect the FMA from accusations that a flaw has occurred in the selection process to the regulatory sandbox. In the Netherlands, no specific legal amendments were performed. Outside of the EU, the regulatory sandboxes in Hong Kong, each operating under the supervision of the various financial supervisors, allow the supervisors to exercise discretion powers, but no newly created set of regulatory sandbox-specific laws or regulations was introduced.

Class waiver – The Australian Securities & Investments Commission (ASIC) has issued a class waiver/FinTech licensing exemption for regulatory sandbox participants. The scope of the waiver is quite wide as the participation in Australia's regulatory sandbox is granted as a matter of law, rather than upon application, and innovation is not a prerequisite. A participant may enjoy the waiver after notifying the ASIC but only for a restricted period, and not all types of services are included in the class waiver (it is unapplicable to issuing financial products or providing credit). In Australia the issuance of the class waiver was within the powers of the ASIC and in accordance with its mandate.

Individual guidance – Innovation hubs often serve the role of a preliminary stage of a regulatory sandbox regime. Innovation hubs provide a dedicated point of contact for firms to raise enquiries with competent authorities and to seek non-binding guidance on regulatory and supervisory expectations, including licensing requirements. On the whole, there are no legal barriers posed by existing laws to the establishment of innovation hubs in EU jurisdictions any many members have established such a hub. The work and mandate of innovation hubs does not differ much from established practices where supervisors respond to queries in a non-binding manner, however jurisdictions have focused on increase the level of technical expertise attached to such hubs as well as designating dedicated teams to the topic. Some competent authorities complement their innovation hubs with specific 'follow-up' schemes. Guidance is a prominent component of most regulatory sandboxes as well. The participation in a regulatory sandbox by construction results in a continuous communication and exchange between participating firms and the supervising authority. Building and enhancing firms' understanding of regulatory expectations, the application of the existing regulatory framework and compliance requirements is one of the objectives of regulatory sandboxes and to achieve it, much communication is needed. Importantly, many developers of financial innovative solutions have a technological background rather than financial background and thus have a low starting point in understanding financial regulation requirements. Increasing the regulator's understanding and knowledge of the innovative products to better assess the risks of new business models and underlying technologies is another important objective, on the side of the supervisor. In the absence of a wide leeway for regulatory alleviations, this property becomes even more central as one of the major benefits and appeals for the participating firms as well as for the supervising authority, from establishing the regulatory sandbox.

In Israel, A pilot regime for FinTech is operated jointly by the Israel Innovation Authority (IIA) and the Israel Securities Authority (ISA). The framework does not offer any regulatory waivers, and general rules apply. The authorisation stage is not part of the regulatory sandbox, and the accepted firm should either enter the test with or without a license, as applicable by existing laws. Regulatory guidance is offered by ISA, if the concerning firm falls within its jurisdiction, and two other supervisors, i.e. the payment systems supervisor and the banks supervisor located withing the Bank of Israel participate as observers. A unique feature of the Israeli test regime is that accepted firms receive financial support for the testing (see further below).

No enforcement action letters – the FCA in the UK has the right to issue a no enforcement action letter stating that no FCA enforcement action will be taken against testing activities. The FCA's commitment not to take enforcement action applies to the period from the issue of the NAL until the testing is completed or closed by the FCA. It is important to note that this only addresses the risk of enforcement action by the FCA and does not limit the Fintech's liability towards its customers. The Bank of Lithuania in its resolution regarding the establishment of a regulatory sandbox has declared that it will not undertake enforcement measures toward financial market participant operating in the regulatory sandbox. In both cases this commitment is not guaranteed and there are some limitations to its implementation in extreme cases.

As a rule of thumb, regulatory sandboxes do not offer any alleviations in the testing environment with regard to regulatory requirements in these three areas (Deloitte, 2017[6]; EBRD, 2019[7]):

- Consumer protections provisions
- Data protection provisions
- Compliance with AML/CFT obligations

In addition, regulatory sandboxes do not offer solutions to several non-regulatory barriers that are often faced by FinTechs and are related to their business models. Participation in a regulatory sandbox does not guarantee the opening of a bank account for the FinTech, a common problem, where banks sometimes decline the opening of a bank account to FinTechs, due to regulatory AML rules applicable to them. Sandboxes, including those that have a focus on data, cannot offer access to individual-level data, because either it will constitute a breach of privacy rules, or in most cases such data is proprietary to incumbents.

Supervisors allow, and even encourage, partnership between large firms (incumbents) and start-ups to apply to the regulatory sandbox, both to foster innovation based on data, and since such joint projects resolve the problem of the FinTech not being licensed, as it can operate as a third party and the incumbent assumes the supervisory obligations. Although obvious, a regulatory sandbox does not guarantee a consumer base for the innovative service or product, which can be a source of failure for the test as well.

A regulatory sandbox can offer financial aid in setting up the test. In Israel, such financial support constitutes one of the major attracting factors of the testing environment, as the regulatory assistance given takes the form of individual guidance and no further. The rate of financial support to the accepted firms varies from 20% to 50% of approved expenses associated with the testing. Financial support at an exceptional rate of 60% of the approved expenses will be given to a programme that has the potential to have an extraordinary impact on streamlining and improving the capital markets or the financial services industries in Israel.

Based on the above experience of other EU and OECD jurisdictions, and the conditions of the Czech FinTech ecosystem, it is recommended that the Czech regulatory sandbox does not provide any waivers; restricted authorisations or other relaxation of existing applicable rules, which would anyway be against EU rules. It is recommended that a proportional application of existing regulatory and supervisory requirements, as embedded in EU financial services regulation, is used as appropriate and at the discretion of the Authorities for firms participating in the Czech regulatory sandbox. Such proportionality can apply to the governance process and system and control requirements, board composition; financial soundness; reputation; management experience and track record (Deloitte, 2017[6]). Proportionality should be applied on a case-by-case basis by the Authorities, depending on the business model and the applicable rules.

2.2.2. Regulatory and supervisory oversight

The recommendation for the Czech regulatory sandbox that would maximise operational benefits, improve the dissemination of regulatory clarity on the one hand, and understanding of business models by the Authorities on the other hand, is to have the regulatory sandbox set up by the Czech Authorities, as per all EU regulatory sandboxes. The experience of these EU regulatory sandboxes has showed that FinTechs benefit from an unmediated exchange of knowledge with the Authorities. This is positive both in terms of the innovators' ability to understand the regulatory and supervisory requirements, but also in terms of the possibility to directly introduce their specifics to the Czech Authorities and thus deepen mutual understanding. No exemptions are to be granted to participating firms in the regulatory sandbox under the licensing procedure beyond those provided by national and European law. There is therefore no need for legislative changes for the establishment of a regulatory sandbox, as the recommended design for the Czech regulatory sandboxes does not involve the disapplication of regulatory obligations that are required to be imposed as a result of EU and/or national law. The Czech Authorities can establish the regulatory sandbox by an internal act or by designating which posts will be dedicated to co-ordinating its operation within the relevant Authorities.

It is recommended that the Czech regulatory sandbox does not provide any form of waivers. Testing in regulatory sandboxes means enabling the provision of innovative financial services in the real market (perhaps in part of the market, depending on the case) under the intensive supervision of the Czech Authorities and in regular consultations with each other, which follows only after obtaining the relevant license. Participants shall benefit from guidance regarding compliance of their activity with applicable regulation and assistance in obtaining license.

It could also be envisaged that a data sandbox without a regulatory component could be outsourced and/or exist outside the Czech Authorities, although even in this alternative the Authorities would need to participate inter alia by means of providing data.

Regular consultations between the participant and the Czech Authorities shall take place throughout the testing phase, during which participants will be required to report on the testing process and any other relevant information. These regular consultations should be co-ordinated by a dedicated regulatory sandbox staff member and are attended by representatives of the Czech Authorities, e.g. representatives from the Financial Market Supervision Department, the Licensing and Sanctions Department, the Regulation and International Co-operation Department or the FinTech team.

The participant must clearly communicate with the users of their financial product that the product is provided in the testing regime of the regulatory sandbox. If a participant fails to comply with the testing plan, the Czech Authorities may use standard mechanisms such as a notice to remedy or, if remedy is not achieved within a specified period of time, a fine.

The regulatory sandbox will also allow the opportunity to get involved in cross-border testing in the EU. For example, the EU Digital Finance Platform will allow multi-sandbox testing in two or more regulatory sandboxes in different Member States, facilitating visibility over the tests among national authorities involved in testing. The cross-border testing is framework is developed by the European Forum for Innovation Facilitators and forms a gateway to regulatory sandbox testing involving multiple national authorities.[3]

It should be noted that competent authorities of other EU countries such as Denmark, Lithuania, the Netherlands and Poland, as well as the UK, have noted their statutory objectives of contributing to financial stability, promoting confidence in the financial sector in their jurisdictions and consumer protection as the foundation for their regulatory sandbox initiatives. As regulatory sandboxes can be used by authorities and firms to gain a good understanding of the opportunities and risks presented by innovations through the testing process, the lessons learned can inform the appropriate regulatory and supervisory response. That response could, for example, take the form of a new set of supervisory rules relating to the disclosure requirements for the sale of a specific new financial product in order to ensure an appropriate degree of protection for consumers or, indeed, a prohibition on the sale of the product if the risk of serious consumer detriment is identified. Given this, the above-mentioned authorities view the regulatory sandbox process no differently from any other tool available to them in developing regulatory and supervisory policies in relation to emerging activities (ESMA, EBA and EIOPA, 2018[8]).

2.2.3. Scope of a regulatory sandbox

The scope of a regulatory sandbox is a critical aspect that determines the flexibility and effectiveness of the framework. The design of the regulatory sandbox for the Czech Republic should be guided by the principles of fostering innovation while ensuring financial stability and consumer protection. The scope of the regulatory sandbox should be clearly defined, taking into account the existing regulatory landscape, the competency of the relevant authorities, and the potential cross-sectoral impacts of new financial technologies.

Typically, the authority's supervisory mission and the characteristics of the domestic financial industry it oversees determine the scope of regulatory sandboxes. However, FinTechs frequently breach the conventional lines separating the various financial services sectors (e.g. financial aggregation platforms) or offer ideas that might increase efficiency horizontally across sectors (e.g. in risk management). Scholars emphasise the unfavorability of sectoral limits because they magnify already-existing regulatory barriers and potentially inhibit cross-sectoral innovation by limiting economies of scale (Parenti, 2020[9]).

The majority of the regulatory sandboxes that are now in use in the EU (Denmark, Hungary, Lithuania, Latvia and Malta) are hosted by an integrated national supervisor, encompassing the whole financial sector (e.g. banking, investment activities and services, insurance). The banking and capital markets supervisors in the Netherlands, which use a "twin peaks" model of financial supervision, collaborate to run the regulatory sandbox. In other countries with sectoral supervisors, one of the regulatory sandboxes planned is a combined operation by all sectoral supervisors (to the extent that this information is accessible, for example, Spain and Italy). With relation to innovation centres, sectoral restrictions show up more frequently, again mostly because of restrictions on the supervisor's authority. In these situations, co-operatively run innovation centres (like Belgium and the Netherlands) have claimed benefits in terms of automated information exchange, an effective method for responding to inquiries, and improved cross-sector issue monitoring. To reduce the danger of creating fragmented cross-sectoral practises, improved regulatory collaboration and methods for information sharing between sectoral regulators are required where such combined operation is not practicable (Parenti, 2020[9]).

It is essential that the eligibility criteria, regulatory sandbox parameters, supervision and oversight, and exit criteria are well-defined while at the same time allow some level of flexibility. A well-defined and flexible scope can ensure that the regulatory sandbox is able to support innovation while also ensuring the protection of consumers and the integrity of the financial system. Last but not least, it is important to bear in mind that the scope of a regulatory sandbox may change over time as the FinTech industry and regulatory environment evolve, and this is why some level of flexibility is important.

Participating institutions from the government should include but are not limited to the Supervisory and Regulatory Authorities. These institutions should consider a range of possibilities for the regulatory sandbox such as, allowing for the testing of new products and services in a controlled environment, identifying relevant regulation for certain activities, and facilitating the development of new technologies and business models.

The design of the regulatory sandbox for the Czech Republic should be guided by the principles of fostering innovation while ensuring financial stability and consumer protection. The scope of the regulatory sandbox should be clearly defined, taking into account the existing regulatory landscape, the competency of the relevant authorities, and the potential cross-sectoral impacts of new financial technologies.

The recommended scope for the Czech regulatory sandbox would be cross-sectoral with no restrictions as to the sector of activity, provided that these fall under the remit of the financial Authorities directly or indirectly. In this context, 'indirectly' refers to any financial activity that may not fall under the definition of an activity requiring a license from the Authorities but may still have an impact on the financial sector. Applicant firms must comply with the eligibility criteria provided below (Section 2.3.2).[4]

Furthermore, the regulatory sandbox could be a 'standard' regulatory sandbox in line with established sandboxes in the EU, and/or could be enhanced with data-sharing capabilities. The recommendation for the Czech regulatory sandbox is to commence with the establishment of the 'standard' regulatory sandbox and, to the extent feasible, enrich it with the provision of data-sharing when the conditions allow it. The conditions for this option will be based on (i) the availability of datasets and ability to make these available; (ii) the capacity of the authorities participating in the regulatory sandbox.

It could also be envisaged that a data sandbox could be established outside the Czech Authorities (and/or outsourced). FinTechs participating in such data sandbox could build data-driven models that would form part of a business model or service and which may not necessarily directly involve financial market activity. However, even in this alternative the Czech Authorities would likely need to participate, *inter alia* by means of providing data.

2.2.4. Underlying legal framework for the operation of the regulatory sandbox

Licensing of financial services, which should be followed for any licensing in the context of the regulatory sandbox

The general regulation that governs the character and course of administrative proceedings in the granting of a license is Act No. 500/2004 Coll., Code of Administrative Procedure, as amended. The procedure and requirements for obtaining a license for a specific type of financial service are laid down in specific sectoral laws.[5] The details of the requirements, annexes, etc. are regulated by the relevant internal acts issued by the Authority to implement the respective laws.

Simplified license

There are certain cases in which Act No. 370/2017 Coll. on Payments (Act on Payments), as amended, which is implementing Payment Services Directive 2 (PSD2),[6] gives a possibility to small-scale payment service providers and small-scale electronic money issuers to be exempted from obligation to have a full license.[7] Instead, it is sufficient to apply for simplified small-scale payment service provider license according to the Section 59 of the Act on Payments and small-scale electronic money issuer license according to the Section 99 of the Act on Payments.

Limited licenses

In certain cases, it is in accordance with Czech law to attach certain restrictions or conditions to the issued license. This possibility is provided in Section 1 (8) of the Act No. 21/1992 Coll., on Banks, as amended, which states that a banking license "shall contain a nominal definition of the permitted activity and may contain a definition of the scope of the permitted activity, but not in the sense of a limitation on the number of individual business cases, and may also contain a determination of the conditions which a bank or a branch of a bank from a non-Member State must meet before commencing any permitted activity or comply with in the performance of any permitted activity." It is important to note that the provision is in direct contradiction with the restricted authorisation principle as mentioned above in the report and therefore the recommended design of the regulatory sandbox is not based on the restricted authorisation principle.

The possibility to attach a restriction or requirement to the approval of a proposed acquisition is in line with European law in relation to licenses related to direct insurance other than life assurance. According to the judgement of the Court of Justice of the European Union on t25 June, 2015, in the case of CO Sociedad de Gestión y Participación SA and Others v De Nederlandsche Bank NV and Others, such restrictions or requirements are in line with the Directive 92/49/EEC on the co-ordination of laws, regulations and administrative provisions relating to direct insurance other than life assurance and its articles 15, 15a and 15b.[8]

As per the exceptions provided for in MIFID II" in Article 2 (c). – transposed into Czech law in the Act No. 256/2004 Coll., Capital Market Business, as amended – "the provision of a principal investment service shall not require authorisation under this Act if the principal investment service is provided (..) by a person providing the main investment service only occasionally, in connection with the exercise of another professional or business activity, provided that there is another legal regulation or code of ethics governing such activities and that regulation provides for the provision of such principal investment service." Thus, if participation in a regulatory sandbox would not be considered a continuous business activity within the meaning of the MIFID II, the persons defined above would not need to obtain authorisation/licensing.

In other areas, it is not possible to grant limited licenses in the Czech Republic under the current legal regulations. For the use of limited licenses within the regulatory sandbox, a new regulation special to the laws that regulate licenses in areas where it is in line with European legislation would be necessary. A similar approach was taken, for example, in the establishment of the Spanish regulatory sandbox (Banco de España, 2022[10]).

Recommended application of supervisory discretion and proportionality in accordance with EU principles

The study of the European Parliament on Regulatory Sandboxes and Innovation Hubs for FinTech notes that while respecting boundaries set by the EU harmonisation, Member States use the exercise of legally embedded levers of proportionality which allow supervisory discretion by considering certain factors, such as the risk profile, or the size, complexity and interconnectedness of the firms concerned (Parenti, 2020[9]). As mentioned above in Section 2.2.1 and 2.2.2, it is recommended that proportionality is applied to participants of the regulatory sandbox, as appropriate and on a case-by-case basis, in accordance with EU applicable regulatory frameworks.

There are examples of the calls for proportional approach, for example Article 74(2) of Directive 2013/36/EU,[9] which is addressed also in Guidelines on internal governance under Directive 2013/36/EU by the European Banking Agency (EBA, 2021[11]).

For example, the Supervisory Authority details general procedures for the exercise of individual discretion with examples of its discretion in relation to Regulation No. 575/2013 on prudential requirements for credit institutions and investment firms (Czech National Bank, n.d.[12]).[10]

For national rules regulating an area not covered by European rules, there is room for discretion only where these laws explicitly allow it. In this area, however, there is room for an internal discussion on the appropriate modification of the legislation for the purpose of establishing a regulatory sandbox. For example, the Czech National Bank has more opportunities to exercise discretion in relation to the general guidelines it has issued itself.[11]

Relevant stakeholders and their required engagement

The establishment of the Czech regulatory sandbox by the Czech Authorities will allow valuable knowledge exchange and meaningful benefits to be reaped for both the applicants and the Authorities. The Czech Authorities shall be the one choosing successful applicants (see Section 2.3.5).

The regulatory sandbox is also an opportunity to build on the good practice of stakeholders' interaction and knowledge sharing through roundtables organised by the FinTech Contact. It is recommended to establish an Advisory Board, which could include representatives of the industry, the Czech National Bank, the Ministry of Finance of the Czech Republic, other representatives of state administration and academia to assess applicants' requests to participate in the regulatory sandbox. In this way, the application of the eligibility criteria can be assessed from multiple perspectives of a diverse Advisory Board.

The authority operating the Czech regulatory sandbox should be able to co-operate with administration agencies that have supervisory responsibilities concerning the participating or applying FinTechs, as far as that administration agency is not represented directly in the sandbox. This can build on the existing co-operation channels between relevant agencies (OECD, 2022[13]).

As innovations are bound to be multifaceted, the list of partners should not be definite, but it is reasonable to engage in communication, namely with the Data Protection Agency and CzechInvest, which can share its recent experience of supporting new business models in its Technology Incubation project (Hořínek, 2022[14]).

Industry Associations can be vital partners in disseminating information on regulatory sandbox among its members and are a valuable source of feedback on the functionalities of the regulatory sandbox. Representatives could provide their expertise in the frame of the Advisory Board.

It is good practice to publish press releases and regular reports on activity of the regulatory sandbox. It is a suitable tool to transparently describe scale and level of the engagement of the Czech Authorities with involved actors, assessing the frequency and depth of the collaboration and consider adjustment of the design of the regulatory sandbox to ensure highest possible efficiency. It is also an opportunity to evaluate the number of applicants and participants of the regulatory sandbox.

2.2.5. Consumer protection and risk management

It is recommended that the Czech regulatory sandbox offers no alleviations to sandbox participants with regard to consumer protection measures stipulated by regulation and supervision and those standard rules apply, aligning with common practice in other regulatory sandboxes. Proportionality considerations are as well usually unapplicable to consumer protection measures. Moreover, there might be restrictions imposed to further protect consumers. Specific measures that can be taken in the regulatory sandbox to protect consumers are shown in Figure 2.4.

Figure 2.4. Consumer protection measures

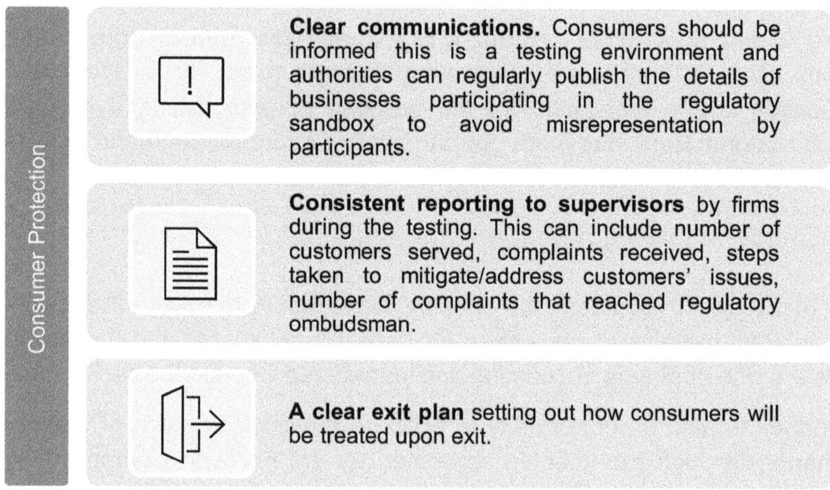

The ESA joint report suggests that compensation or redress measures accompany the regulatory sandbox should any detriment be suffered in the context of testing (ESMA, EBA and EIOPA, 2019[2]). This is a beneficial measure for consumers and if taken, will mean that less intense communication efforts to convey the associated risk of the test is needed. However, if firms bear all the risks, this could make the regulatory sandbox too expensive for small firms.

The FCA considered several compensation options before launching the first test cohort, with options ranging from no compensation offered and consumers knowingly consenting, to setting a condition for joining the regulatory sandbox that businesses undertake to compensate any losses (including investment losses) to customers and can demonstrate that they have the resources in place to cover such compensations. In the interim options, the FCA considered relying on the UK's Financial Services Compensation Scheme (FSCS) that provides a broad compensation, covering claims in relation to deposits, investment business, home finance, insurance policies and insurance broking, provided by businesses authorised by the FCA and the Prudential Regulation Authority (PRA). However, the FCA, not wanting firms to bear the costs of paying fees to the Financial Ombudsman Service (FOS) and the FSCS decided to follow a case-by-case basis framework of setting the disclosure, protection, and compensation appropriate to the testing activity (FCA, 2015[15]).

In contrast, Switzerland has limited safeguards for the regulatory sandbox participants that according to the local set up are not authorised while they operate as restricted services, and these firms are not covered by the compensation scheme (EBRD, 2019[7]). In Australia, the ASIC has set requirements for adequate compensation arrangements: a professional indemnity insurance policy with a minimum CAD 1 million limit for any one claim and aggregated claims; and requiring the business to take reasonable steps to obtain run-off cover for a period of 12 months.

Under EU regulation, payment service providers, electronic money institutions and payment account information administrators are required to provide an insurance contract or a comparable guarantee as a prerequisite for getting a licence for payment initiation or account information service provision. Because the proposed Czech regulatory sandbox will not offer regulatory waivers, the compensation and consumer protection measure set in each license type should provide the appropriate protection so that all consumers can be offered the product. If the regulator assesses that extraordinary risks are associated with a particular test, it can use a consumer suitability test and allow only sophisticated/accredited/non-retail consumers to participate. Alternatively, it can demand a clear consent of consumers to use the service, expressing agreement to the risks.

In many regulatory sandboxes risk identification and mitigation measures are included as part of the eligibility criteria (Bromberg, Godwin and Ramsay, 2017[16]). In cases where a restricted licence or a waiver is offered, businesses or individuals might seek to use their participation in a regulatory sandbox as a means of legitimising their unlicensed schemes. In EU member states, regulatory sandboxes where no exemptions from the authorisation process are offered to participants, there should not be additional layers of risk other than the ones addressed and monitored by the supervisor for all supervised activities. In the case of Australia, ASIC's industry licensing exemption has attracted the objections of consumer groups.

Most regulatory sandbox arrangements do not require that applicants use a particular technology to be accepted to the sandbox. A regulatory sandbox is a technology neutral solution (EBRD, 2019[7]). However, as regulatory sandboxes are set up with the objective to test a product, service, or business model it is expected in application criteria that the level of development of the business model and the underlying technology is sufficiently advanced to begin the testing. The regulatory sandbox supervisory and guiding team relies most often on the staff of the financial supervisor. Industry and technology experts are usually not part of this team, if anything, they have a role in the selection phase to the testing environment. An innovation hub is a more appropriate venue than a regulatory sandbox for firms that are still struggling to find the technological solution for their product.

Access to data is one of the attributes to be considered in the design recommendations of this feasibility study. Indeed, a considerable part of Czech FinTechs use data and access to data has the potential to foster more innovation. However, financial data at customer or SME level (such as banking or transactional data) contains personally identifiable information and is subject to strict obligations under GDPR.

Providing access to public data, test data, anonymised data or synthetic data are the possible options to overcome issues of data security and privacy. The FCA has so far been the only regulatory sandbox to include micro level data, real and public, or synthetic for FinTechs to test on. FinTechs have expressed high demand for the data though it is not without drawbacks (see Section 1.4).

The FCA conducted legal analysis and concluded that there is not a sufficient legal basis for its regulatory sandbox to make large volumes of real personal data available for FinTechs. Further, the FCA has decided so far against using pseudonymised and anonymised data assessing that the privacy risk remains considerable. The FCA therefore chose to generate and make available synthetic data to their regulatory sandbox participants (FCA, 2021[17]).

When developing the framework for the EU Digital Finance Platform's Data hub, it was considered to use companies' credits, loans and balance sheet information available to the European Commission (EC). However, many members of the EFIF warned the EC that this information (particularly the loan and credit data sets) was highly confidential/sensitive and could not be shared with third parties due to legal reasons. For that reason, a preliminary stage in the development of the data hub became the synthetic data pilot in Spain (Dirección General de Estabilidad Financiera et al., 2022[18]).

Within the pilot environment, the FCA provided data that could be accessed either via an API or through an integrated Jupyter Notebook (enabling to process and analyse large volumes of data) (FCA, 2021[17]).

2.2.6. Legislative changes

The main benefits of the recommended design of the regulatory sandbox relate to strengthened co-operation and increased level of assistance of the Czech Authorities to entrepreneurs in obtaining a licence, emphasis on the use of the current possibilities of proportional access and intensive exchange of knowledge. The proposed regulatory sandbox design could be launched within the framework of the current legislative framework and does not require a new law to be established, as it does not deviate from existing EU law and does not envisage the offering of any kind of waivers or exemptions. A proportional application of regulatory and supervisory requirements, as embedded in EU regulation, should be used appropriately and at the discretion of the Authorities.

If, after the first years of the operation of the regulatory sandbox, it is assessed that a beneficial option would be to use a restricted authorisation model or to introduce rule waivers, class waivers or no enforcement action letters, it would be necessary to enshrine such options in a legislative change. Equally, implications of the local legal framework of the Czech Republic (e.g. administrative law provisions and implications of public law for the implementation) are not being analysed in this report. Such legal advice can be obtained by the Czech Authorities from competent parties should they require such an assessment.

2.3. Recommended process flow and implementation guidance

The recommended process flow is illustrated in Figure 2.5, and the various stages are elaborated on in detail in the following subsections, including the recommended risk register, the application eligibility criteria, the authorisation model, the licensing procedure, and limits to the testing environment.

Figure 2.5. Schematic representation of the recommended process flow

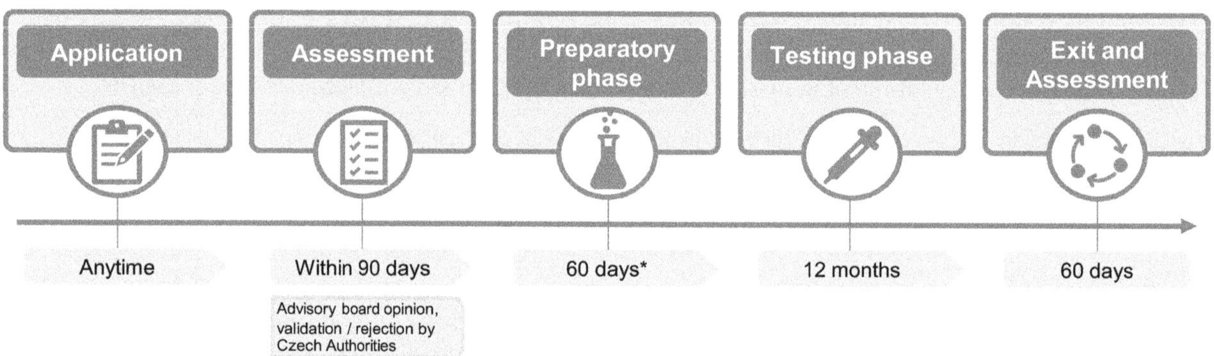

Note: (*) if there is no need for authorisation, otherwise the duration is determined by licensing timelines.

2.3.1. Recommended risk register

The operation of the regulatory sandbox should monitor whether a tested activity or service may result in the exacerbation of systematic or reputation risks or harm competition in the financial services sector. It is recommended that the sandbox keeps a risk register where the activity of participants is evaluated, and the following risks can be mitigated:

CGAP suggests that products and services that are tested in a regulatory sandbox may present additional risks that may be hard to assess before the innovation is fully launched in the market. These risks may include those stemming from features of the innovation and/or limited regulatory and supervisory capacity. Such a systematic risk can be prevented by well-designed regulatory requirements and adequate supervisory tools necessary for collecting and analysing the data generated or used by new technologies (Jenik and Lauer, 2017[19]).

Liability issues may arise in case of failed testing that results in harm to customers or other market participants in the case of regulatory sandboxes, which allow significant exceptions to the standard licensing regime. Such a situation would threaten the reputation of the regulator and trust of customers in the financial system. This risk is unapplicable with regard to the framework recommended for the Czech Republic, because no exceptions form the licensing regime are offered to FinTechs under this set of recommendations. Resolution and compensation measures for consumer are already in place with regard to licensed entities as per the standard applicable frameworks. On the Authority's side, early termination is covered (see Section 2.3.7) if it realises that there is higher than expected risk to consumers or the financial sector stemming from the tested product/service or if fraud or any other similar shortcomings arise, in the same way that a license can be revoked under regular conditions.

Risks may also result from the lack of consumers' understanding of a new product. Transparent communication of the specifics of the regulatory sandbox are needed to realistically adjust expectations.

Advice and support of the participant may be seen as a disruptor to the competition. Clear, not overly vague, selection criteria are providing transparency in order to avoid selection bias.

Possible limited capacity of regulator in terms of adequate resources of staff and funding may lead to following risk of poor selection of participants of the regulatory sandbox caused by the limited capacity of the regulator to assess the innovation. Moreover, overburdened staff which would be given extra duties in the frame of a regulatory sandbox instead of creating a new dedicated regulatory sandbox unit, there is a risk of insufficient capacity to address the main regulator's responsibilities. Therefore, it is necessary to sufficiently assess the necessary number and skillset of dedicated personnel.

2.3.2. Eligibility criteria

The recommended criteria to be met by applicant firms wishing to be admitted to the Czech regulatory sandbox include (Table 2.3): The regulatory sandbox applicant offers an innovative financial product, service, business model or solution; the product brings benefits to users of financial services in the Czech Republic; the product is ready for market launch so that testing in a regulatory sandbox is feasible and safe; there is a specific need for testing of the product; the applicant is of good character; responsible management of personal data is ensured; the applicant commits to investor protection and compliance; and there is direct or indirect relevance to the Authority running the regulatory sandbox. It is recommended that participants in the regulatory sandbox hold the appropriate license for the regulated activity undertaken or are ready to apply for a license in order to have a license before the start of the testing phase, if the Authority deems that the activity falls within the perimeter of regulated financial activity.

In particular, the following eligibility criteria, which are based on good practice of the regulatory sandboxes of EU Member States, are recommended for the Czech regulatory sandbox in more detail:

The regulatory sandbox applicant offers an innovative product, service, or business strategy that makes use of novel or developing technologies to offer fresh or enhanced financial services in the Czech marketplace, including a new adaptation or material improvement of another financial product, service, business model or solution. A product, service, or business model that makes use of current technology in new or creative ways will also be referred to as an innovative financial product.

The product brings benefits to users of financial services in the Czech Republic and these benefits are identifiable e.g. it offers a different solution from other offerings on the Czech financial market, an enhancement of an existing product, service, business model or solution, a more inclusive business model or a solution that increases the efficiency of financial institutions or markets, etc.

The product is ready for market launch so that testing in a regulatory sandbox is feasible and safe if the applicant has a clear idea of what it expects from its participation in the regulatory sandbox (applicant is capable to specify a concrete testing target) and the company has sufficient staff and financial resources and capacity to ensure its operations and the provision of the relevant financial service. It includes readiness to handle testing technically (the product has appropriate and sufficiently robust and resilient ICT infrastructure and mechanisms for data security and against cyber-attacks), deal with risks that may arise during testing (i.e. analyse these potential risks in advance and prepare mitigation measures), and – importantly – readiness of the company to meet regulatory requirements. The latter means that the company is either a licensed company or ready to apply for a license in order to have a license before the start of the testing phase, if the license is deemed necessary according to the Czech Authorities. In case the Authorities deem that a license is not necessary, the Czech Authorities have the discretion to allow the company to perform the testing or not.

There is a specific need for testing of the product for example in case that there is an existing controversy or ambiguity about applicable law that would otherwise prevent the standard launch of the product or a there is a need to test the product in a limited form before it is fully launched.

The criterion of good character is demonstrated by clean criminal record of the applicant.

Responsible management of personal data is likely to be ensured if the Data Protection Authority does not identify high level of risk of unlawful processing of personal data or unlawful interference with the rights and freedoms of data subjects during the testing.

Commitment to investor protection and compliance can be demonstrated by mitigation mechanisms incorporated in the business plan.

The activity is directly or indirectly covered by the financial legislation.

The business model is relevant to the Authority running the regulatory sandbox.

Table 2.3. Recommended eligibility criteria for the Czech regulatory sandbox

Eligibility criteria	To be accepted	Not to be accepted
The regulatory sandbox applicant offers an **innovative** financial product, service, business model or solution	The applicant adequately explains how their good, service, or business strategy that makes use of novel or developing technologies to offer fresh or enhanced financial services is considered to be new and original in the Czech marketplace, including a new adaptation or material improvement of another financial product, service, business model or solution. A product, service, or business model that makes use of current technology in new or creative ways will also be referred to as an innovative financial product.	The applicant will not be accepted with the financial product, service, business model or solution that are offered in the Czech Republic by other companies and does not offer any enhancement or does not makes use of current technology in new or creative way
The product brings **benefits** to users of financial services **in the Czech Republic**	The innovation may bring clearly identifiable positive impacts on its users such as direct impact (cheaper offers, greater variety of offers, accessibility) or indirect impacts (solutions increasing efficiency and reducing back-office costs).	The innovation does not seem to bring clearly identifiable positive impacts on its users.
The **product is ready for market launch** so that testing in a regulatory sandbox is feasible and safe	Technological readiness: Technology Readiness Levels (TRLs) are a method for understanding the technical maturity of a technology.[1] The applicant shall be able to reach at least TRL 4.	Technological readiness: The applicant does not reach at least TRL 4.
	The applicant must provide a sound and viable business plan.	The applicant does not have a clear idea on business case of its innovation.
	The applicant ready to start the licensing procedure within reasonable time upon consultation with Czech Authorities, in case it is deemed that a license is necessary for proposed innovation.	The applicant is not ready for the licensing procedure, and it needs more time to be ready for consultation with Czech Authorities in order to be able to submit relevant application for an authorisation.
There is a specific **need for testing** of the product	The applicant analysed relevant legislation and their innovation raises questions about the correct application of relevant legislation.	The application did not do legal analyses related to the innovation and/or regulation does not raise major questions.

Eligibility criteria	To be accepted	Not to be accepted
	The applicant shall list their expectation from testing their financial product or service and plans to exit the regulatory sandbox.	The applicant is not able to identify benefits of the testing for their innovation.
The applicant is of a good **character**	The applicant has a clean criminal record.	The applicant does not have a clean criminal record.
Responsible management of **personal data**	The applicant is ready to demonstrate their mechanism to ensure responsible management of personal data in line with the respective legislation.	The applicant does not have mechanisms to ensure responsible management of personal data in line with the respective legislation in place.
Commitment to **investor/consumer protection** and compliance	The applicant can outline their plan on investor/consumer protection and has sufficient financial and human resources that enable them to act on it during the testing.	The applicant is not able to outline their plan on investor/consumer protection and/or does not have sufficient financial and human resources to be able to act on it during the testing.
The activity is directly or indirectly covered by the financial legislation	The innovation involves a financial service or product. The financial regulation covers the activity.	The innovation is not a financial service or product. The financial regulation does not cover the activity.

1. https://ec.europa.eu/research/participants/data/ref/h2020/wp/2014_2015/annexes/h2020-wp1415-annex-g-trl_en.pdf

Table 2.4. Eligibility criteria in regulatory sandboxes established in EU countries

Eligibility criteria:	**Eligibility criteria in regulatory sandboxes of following countries:**
The regulatory sandbox applicant offers an innovative financial product, service, business model or solution	DK, HU, LT, LV, NL, MT BG, CY, EE, EL, ES, HR, IE, PT, RO, SK, AT
The product brings benefits to users of financial services in domestic market	DK, HU, LT, LV, NL, MT BG, EE, EL, ES, HR, PT, SK
The product is ready for market launch so that testing in a regulatory sandbox is feasible and safe	Test readiness: DK, HU, LT, NL, MT ES, IE, PT, SK, AT
There is a specific need for testing of the product	Risk mitigation: NL, EE, EL, AT
The applicant is of good character	DK, LT, NL, MT BG, HR, PT, SK
Responsible management of personal data	SK
Commitment to investor protection and compliance	There are a number of regulatory sandboxes focused solely on data protection.
The activity is directly or indirectly covered by the financial legislation	CY, EL

Source: Based on the European Parliament (2020[9]), Regulatory Sandboxes and Innovation Hubs for FinTech, https://www.europarl.europa.eu/RegData/etudes/STUD/2020/652752/IPOL_STU(2020)652752_EN.pdf.Source: Based on Regulatory Sandboxes and Innovation Hubs for FinTech and updated; https://www.europarl.europa.eu/RegData/etudes/STUD/2020/652752/IPOL_STU(2020)652752_EN.pdf

The above recommended eligibility criteria have been formed taking into account the experience of other EU countries and the specific characteristics of the Czech FinTech ecosystem.

Technological readiness

For regulatory sandboxes to be effective, it is essential that the technology used to track and observe stakeholder participants is robust, reliable and up-to-date. In the design of a regulatory sandbox for the Czech Republic, technology readiness is an important consideration (.

Figure 2.6). It is recommended that firms that become eligible for participation in the Czech regulatory sandbox have a Technology Readiness Levels of at least TRL 4, so that there is a proof of concept tested in a lab setting.[12]

Figure 2.6. Technological readiness

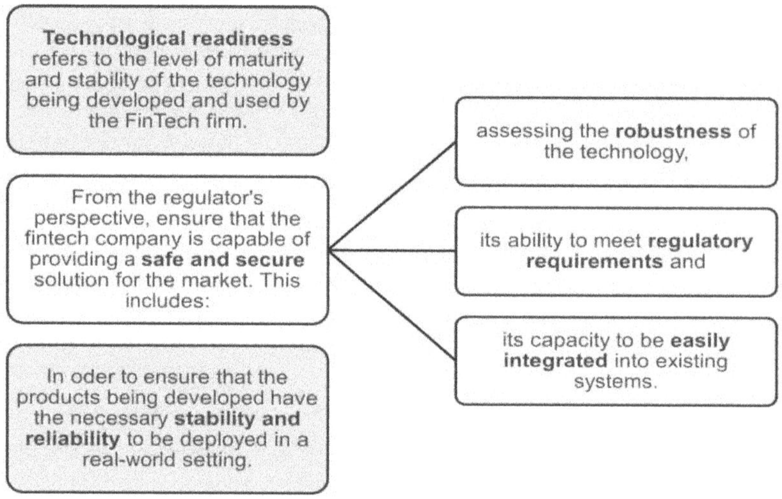

Technology Readiness Levels (TRLs) are widely used in the technology industry to help management make informed decisions on the advancement and deployment of technology. TRLs offer several benefits when used in the design of a regulatory sandbox. Firstly, they provide a common understanding of the state of technology, allowing stakeholders to assess the maturity and readiness of a particular financial innovation. Secondly, they help in managing risks by providing a clear understanding of the technology's development journey and its potential for successful deployment. In the third place, the regulator should take into account the technology's stability and scalability. These evaluations are required to establish a strong foundation and guarantee the success of the testing procedure. Israel, for example, requires a TRL6 in its regulatory sandbox (Israel Innovation Authority, n.d.[20]).

There are, however, some limitations in the usefulness of TRLs. For example, there is no direct correlation between the readiness and the appropriateness or technological development of a product. The regulator has to take into account the compliance with current systems and regulations, and validate the ethical dimension of the technology (see Table 2.5).

Table 2.5. EU Definitions of technology readiness levels

Technology Readiness Level (EU)	Definition
TRL1	Basic principles observed
TRL2	Technology concept formulated
TRL3	Experimental proof of concept
TRL4	Technology validated in lab
TRL5	Technology validated in relevant environment (industrially relevant environment in the case of key enabling technologies)
TRL6	Technology demonstrated in relevant environment
TRL7	System prototype demonstration in operational environment
TRL8	System complete and qualified
TRL9	Actual system proven in operational environment (competitive manufacturing in the case of key enabling technologies)

Source: Extract from Part 19 of the Commission Decision C(2014)4995 from the European Commission (2020[21]), Technology readiness levels (TRL), https://ec.europa.eu/research/participants/data/ref/h2020/wp/2014_2015/annexes/h2020-wp1415-annex-g-trl_en.pdf.

One of the key elements of technology readiness in a regulatory sandbox is the ability to accurately track and observe the participants, including the ability to identify and verify the identity of the participating

FinTech companies and their customers, as well as the ability to monitor and record the transactions and activities that take place within the regulatory sandbox. It is necessary the use of robust and reliable technology, such as blockchain and artificial intelligence, which can ensure that data is securely and accurately recorded and can be easily accessed by the regulator.

Another important aspect of technology readiness in a regulatory sandbox is the ability to ensure that the technology used is up-to-date. In order to do this, the technology used in the regulatory sandbox must be continuously tested and monitored so as to spot and fix any problems that may occur. To make sure the technology is appropriate for the task at hand, it might be necessary to use simulations and involve the participation of experts in the field.

In the third place, a critical aspect of technology readiness is the ability to ensure that the data collected is protected and secure. This is especially important in the Czech Republic, where data protection laws are strong and regulations are strict. To ensure compliance, it is essential to implement robust data security measures, such as encryption and multi-factor authentication, to protect the data collected from unauthorised access or breaches.

When it comes to the leadership of the implementation of the regulatory sandbox, it is important that the responsible entity is well equipped to handle the complex technical and regulatory issues that may arise. The responsible entity could be a dedicated unit within the financial regulator or a separate body with a mandate to oversee the regulatory sandbox. It should have the necessary resources and expertise to oversee the operation of the regulatory sandbox, monitor the progress of the participants, and provide guidance on regulatory issues. Additionally, close collaboration with international regulatory bodies and other regulatory sandbox initiatives in other countries should be established to exchange information and best practices.

2.3.3. Licensing procedure

It is recommended that, as in other EU member countries, the Czech regulatory sandbox does not waive licensing requirements or requirements under the national or EU legislation, and does not offer any alleviation to sandbox participants that cannot be granted as part of the normal authorisation process. To the extent that an applicant is pursuing an activity that requires authorisation, it will be subject to the same supervisory framework as applies to authorised firms in general. A license should be obtained before applying to the regulatory sandbox or it can be obtained at the application stage. In case that during the preparatory phase, the Czech Authorities assesses that the innovation of the applicant does not need the license, it can decide that the testing in the regulatory sandbox would nevertheless be beneficial and prepare the testing plan for the testing phase.

The UK allows a license to be obtained after admission to the regulatory sandbox but prior to commencement of the test as well. The supervisor may assist in the application, and often that is the case. If the firm has been accepted to the regulatory sandbox than that means that the supervisor has recognised that it offers a true innovative product and has the potential to contribute to consumer benefit, then this makes for the rationalisation of assisting the firm to receive authorisation. In fact, firms tend to see, often mistakenly, that the regulatory sandbox is a faster track to authorisation. If the supervisor plans to increase the supervisory resources, it allocates to the regulatory sandbox compared with the regular authorisation track than perhaps a faster process might be achieved. Regardless of the timeframe, all regulatory rules will continue to apply. The use of proportionality as discussed in Section 2.2.1 is the only leeway available to the supervisor in terms of the requirements from the firm to receive the license.

An alternative situation might be where the Czech Authorities are not sure whether the activity sought by the applicant fits within one of the existing license regimes. In this case there is much potential added value for the supervisor if this firm is accepted into the test, because it will give the Czech Authorities an opportunity to get a better understanding of the business model. In the end of the test phase, the Czech

Authorities might have a clearer understanding of how the law applies to this activity, and whether a license is appropriate. Often, FinTechs seek authorisation as they see this as a way to legitimise their business and prefer to have a license even when they might not necessary require one by law. In particular in this group, we should consider firms where a legislation is underway, whether at the EU or national level and a firm that might soon be opt for authorisation is applying (for example the upcoming Markets in Crypto-Assets (MiCA) Regulation).

A possible type of applicants might be partnerships between established companies and third-party FinTechs. The licensed incumbent might seek such participation to avert the risk of pursuing an activity which is outside of its current license scope. If funding or data are also offered for participants, this will increase the attractiveness for incumbents. For the supervisor, the authorised incumbent will need to bear any regulatory requirements, but as it is already accustomed with supervision, it will already have most or all safeguards in place. In the FCA regulatory sandboxes such partnerships have participated, whereas in Austria so far there have not been applications of this form. In the first two cohorts of the FCA regulatory sandbox, partnerships between large firms and start-ups have proven to be successful for both parties, particularly for giving the start-up access to a larger pool of existing customers to test with (FCA, 2017[22]). FinTechs are also able to leverage the resources, experience, and knowledge of the large firm. Before launching their digital sandbox, 56% of participants stated they intended to collaborate with at least one other team in the cohort. Participants stated that the adjacent nature of their solutions meant there would be valuable learning opportunities and the potential for partnerships (FCA, 2021[17]). In Israel such co-operation is encouraged and several incumbents have made public on the test website what is the problem they are looking for a technological solution to. The co-operation might thus arise within the test framework, with the regulatory sandbox offering the motivation for both parts.

2.3.4. Application

To the extent possible, it is recommended that application be performed in a digital manner with as much of the documents having a predefined structure.

The following information has been identified as common in the application and appropriate for the objectives of the Czech regulatory sandbox:

a. Contact and identification details
b. License status, regulatory requirements, regulatory gaps
c. The business plan, description of the product, management competence, potential customer segment, firm financial capabilities, market competitors, potential for expansion abroad, market entry boundaries, expected market impact, what is the innovation
d. The need to enter the test
e. The outline of the test, including measurable milestones during the testing (technological and business)
f. Intellectual property aspects related to the tested product or service
g. a description of the key risks of the proposed test (to both consumers and the Applicant's business) and how the Applicant intends to mitigate these
h. Underlying technology, development level
i. An exit plan
j. An outline of the applicant's next steps if the test is successful.

2.3.5. Authorisation model for assessment

It is recommended that participants in the Czech regulatory sandbox be preselected by a special Advisory Board that will provide a non-binding opinion. This will then be validated or rejected by the Czech Authorities, not applying to the CNB, as the CNB has no legal basis to issue such a decision. The Advisory Board could for example comprise of representatives of the industry, academia, the Czech National Bank, the Ministry of Finance of the Czech Republic, Ministry of Industry and Trade, CzechInvest and Data Protection Agency. It would give a chance to consider multiple angles in relation to the eligibility criteria. It is reasonable to ensure diversity of the Advisory Board to maximise the positive effect of exchange of views and experience in relation to assessed business models. The CNB and the MFCR can provide their expertise in the context of the Advisory Board.

The exact design of the functioning of the Advisory Board should be chosen on the basis of a discussion between the regulatory sandbox implementer and the potential members to best reflect their specific ideas of involvement and capacity to ensure the effective functioning of the Advisory Board.

2.3.6. Preparatory phase

After the application has been evaluated and the applicant has been selected, the applicant is notified and allocated to the contact person in the regulatory sandbox. The selection is followed by the preparatory phase, during which the contact person prepares a testing plan together with the applicant. This plan determines how the testing will be carried out and the participant commits to its performance in the testing plan. The testing plan may include the length and rules of the testing, any restrictions, such as a maximum number of customers to be served, safeguards to protect users of the innovative financial service (e.g. the obligation to inform the user that the product is currently being tested in a regulatory sandbox, the obligation to obtain informed consent from the user, or the obligation to provide evidence of insurance to cover any potential damages the user may incur). The testing plan may specify a level of proportionality which the Czech Authorities may decide to exercise (supervisory discretion by considering certain factors, such as the risk profile, or the size, complexity and interconnectedness of the firms concerned) (Parenti, 2020[9]). The testing shall focus on the compliance of the financial innovation with the relevant regulation (i.e. regulatory aspects of innovative financial services, such as the adequacy of the existing regulation), the existence of any unexpected risks (which would be eliminated after their identification by the Czech Authorities) and the practical implementation of the financial innovation on the market (i.e. whether the product is in demand among users, whether the business model is well set up etc.). The test plan clarifies the expectations of the actors, it is for consideration whether there is a sufficient basis to make it legally binding. Testing on the basis of such a test plan is beneficial for both Authorities, who have the opportunity to learn from close observation of a potentially interesting innovation, and innovators, who have the opportunity to discuss their business model with Authorities and ensure its maximum compliance with relevant regulations.

2.3.7. Exit procedures: early and planned

It is recommended that firms applying to the Czech regulatory sandbox should produce an exit plan, accepted by the Authorities that would allow the orderly termination of the test at any point in time. Upon termination, a report by the firm should be submitted analysing the results and the experience in the regulatory sandbox. Early termination should remain an option both for the participating firms and the Authorities. For the firm such option should be available in case the business model turns-out as insufficient, and for the Authorities, if it comes to the conclusion that the activity poses any risk to financial stability or higher than expected risk to consumers, in the same way that a license can be revoked under regular conditions.

ESA proscribes that regulatory sandbox-participating firms should be required to develop plans to provide for a controlled exit from regulatory sandboxes, including to ensure an appropriate degree of protection for consumers, with either the continuation or discontinuation of the test propositions (ESMA, EBA and EIOPA, 2019[2]). The UK, Singapore and Hong Kong require regulatory sandbox participants to develop an exit plan to ensure the test can be terminated at any time with minimal damage to consumers (EBRD, 2019[7]). In the Netherlands, authorised financial institutions *may* be required to draw up an exit strategy envisaging an orderly market exit when entering the regulatory sandbox. For new market entrants (entity without (the correct) authorisation) it is *required* to provide an exit plan. The components of the exit plan should include, among others: triggers for exit; exit procedures; essential functions that will need to continue; communications plan; describe how ongoing customer relationships will be wound up. In Lithuania applicants need to show an activity termination plan which is to be applied if, following the exit from the regulatory sandbox, service provision will be terminated. In addition, FinTech applicants need to describe the actions to be taken after a successful exit from the regulatory sandbox to further develop the tested financial innovation.

Further, in frameworks where a waiver or a restricted licence is offered to participants, the termination of the testing phase usually implies that the testing firm cannot continue operating under this regime anymore and a full license, if applicable, is required (Australia). If the firm complies with the full license requirements it can broad the scope of the offered services.

Upon exit or termination of the test, authorities often request the participating firms to draw and submit a summarising report. In the UK, the report should include the lessons learned from the test, and how any deficiencies are to be dealt with. The report will include the description of the test and its main attributes, results and next steps for the business. The FCA also asks for participants feedback regarding their experience within the FCA regulatory sandbox and often publishes an analysis report for different cohorts of the regulatory sandbox, in particular if major changes were introduced to the framework, such as adding access to data. Good level of record keeping might be useful for an efficient analysis of the test. It is possible to consider requiring firms to submit interim reports for this purpose. In Israel, due to the financial support provided to the test, the IIA will conduct a financial and technological audit, at the end of which a final accounting will be carried out.

Early exit is usually available in reviewed sandboxes (see Annex D). In particular, this option is allowed in cases where the firm realises there is no consumer uptake. On the Authority's side, early termination might be needed if it realises that there is higher than expected risk to consumers or the financial sector stemming from the tested product/service or if fraud or any other similar shortcomings arise, in the same way that a license can be revoked under regular conditions. The Bank of Lithuania mentions in addition that admission to its regulatory sandbox may be revoked if during its participation in the regulatory sandbox the participant fails to meet the testing conditions indicated in the testing plan (The Bank of Lithuania, 2018[23]).

2.3.8. Recommended timelines

The willingness of policy makers and supervisors to establish testing environment goes hand in hand with the recognition that supervision and authorisation process are often perceived by FinTechs as a barrier for growth. FinTechs operate in a competitive environment over funding, that can be of scarce supply, and due to their small and young nature, do not usually enjoy much internal disposable funding. Their effort is concentrated on completing as quick as possible the development and deployment of their product (time-to-market) to attract more funding. Bearing this objective in mind, it is recommended as a prerequisite for the Czech regulatory sandbox in order to attract demand by FinTechs, that the application and authorisation timelines be attractive.

As for the testing phase, the timeframes vary from 6 to 24 months. In the Netherlands, Hong Kong and Singapore testing timeframe is determined on a case-by-case basis (EBRD, 2019[7]). Time frame can usually be extended following a request by the firm. Alternatively, the competent authority has the power to terminate a test, or a firm may stop the testing through an orderly exit.

The main stages of the testing process that require setting a timeline are the following:

a. The application stage – is application to the regulatory sandbox continuously available or are there specific predefined and restricted time intervals throughout the year when firms can apply.
b. The time from the end of the application period until a decision on participation is communicated to the firm. As recommended, there will be a continuous option to apply for the regulatory sandbox, the time limits for this stage will depend on the frequency of gathering of the advisory board. We suggest the time for this stage not to exceed 90 days.
c. The consecutive stage is to allow the authority and the firm to construct a detailed testing plan. We propose 60 days for this phase. If the company is not already licensed and during the construction of the testing plan the Czech Authorities advises the company to apply for a specific license, this stage, including the licensing procedure will be determined by the administrative rules.
d. The testing phase itself when the firm is offering its products to customers, as applicable. We propose 12 months as is frequent in other regulatory sandboxes, with options both for an early exit and an extension.
e. The ending phase where usually the firm is required to draft and submit a report analysing the results of the test, and for the regulator to inform the firm of any restrictions that may be lifted, or imposed, to receive a full license, if applicable. We propose 60 days for this phase.

2.3.9. Measurement of performance

Regulators should have a clear understanding of how success will be measured in the regulatory sandbox. This can be achieved by identifying Key Performance Indicators (KPIs) and using feedback loops to continuously improve the supervisory approach. It is advisable for regulators to focus on principles-based regulation rather than rules-based regulation, as this will allow them to regulate the activity rather than the entity. Additionally, effective communication with the market is crucial. Some regulators have established dedicated webpages as regulatory sandbox portals to increase awareness, share relevant documents, and provide information to companies (World Bank, 2020[24]). The recommended set of KPIs for the Czech regulatory sandbox are presented in Figure 2.7.

Figure 2.7. Recommended set of KPIs

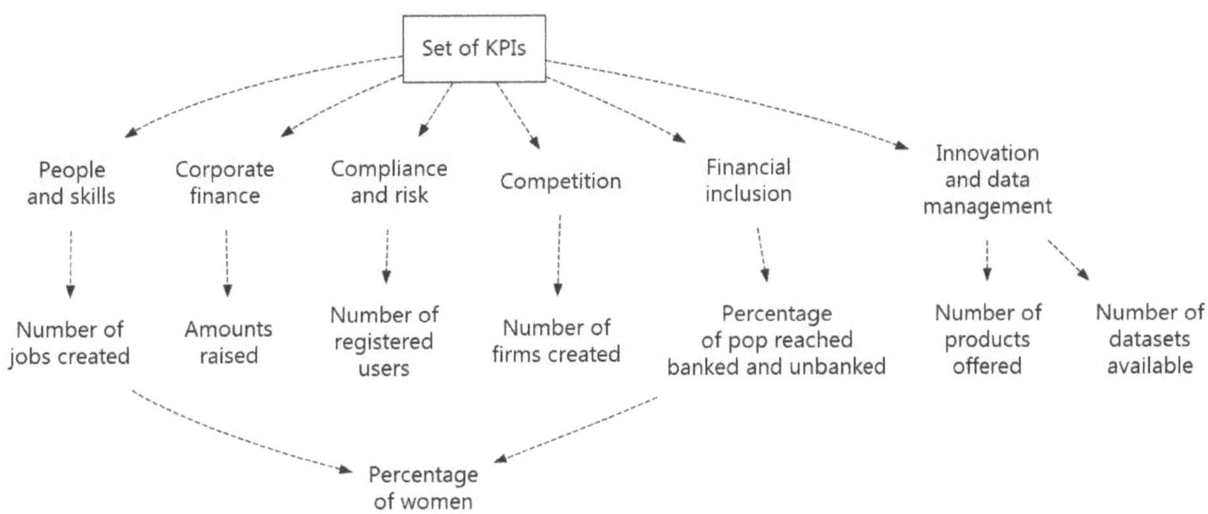

Having KPIs for monitoring a regulatory sandbox for FinTechs is essential in measuring the success of the sandbox, as it helps to determine if the sandbox is meeting its objectives. By selecting the right KPIs, regulators can effectively track progress, measure success, and make necessary adjustments to their regulatory approach. The KPIs selected for a regulatory sandbox should depend on the objectives of the regulatory sandbox. Possible categories of KPIs include people and skills, corporate finance, compliance and risk, competition, financial inclusion, and innovation and data management, provide a comprehensive picture of the impact of the regulatory sandbox. For instance, measuring the number of jobs created and the amount of money raised by FinTechs in the regulatory sandbox can help assess the contribution of the sandbox to facilitating and speeding up the deployment of innovation, and attracting FinTechs locally and globally. The number of registered users and of firms created can measure the regulatory sandbox's impact on competition and adoption of new technologies, while the percentage and characteristics of the population reached can provide insight into the sandbox's contribution to financial inclusion. Finally, the number of products available and the number of datasets available can demonstrate the regulatory sandbox's success in fostering innovation and effective data management. These KPIs provide a comprehensive picture of the regulatory sandbox's impact on various stakeholders and help regulators determine if the sandbox is meeting its objectives.

2.4. Communication strategy

A clear and effective communication strategy is essential for the success of a regulatory sandbox for FinTechs. The communication plan should outline the methods and channels to be used to interact with different stakeholders such as FinTech companies, regulators, and consumers. The communication strategy for the Czech Regulatory Sandbox should aim to build trust and transparency between all stakeholders, foster collaboration and co-operation, and ensure that the goals of the regulatory sandbox are clearly communicated and understood by all.

The recommended communication strategy for the Czech regulatory sandbox should include various layers to ensure effective communication with interested parties (see Figure 2.8). The strategy could be built on the established contact point which has already channels and experience in providing assistance, answering questions, and offering support to FinTechs. A dedicated website is recommended to be established to disseminate information about the regulatory sandbox, including scope and objectives, rules and eligibility criteria, updates and news, and possibly the answers to questions submitted by interested firms for guidance of others. A dedicated email address or mailbox is recommended to also be created to handle inquiries and questions from the participants, the public, and other stakeholders. Additional tools to be considered include newsletters that can be sent periodically to subscribers and interested parties to provide updates and promote awareness of the regulatory sandbox. A framework for communication and sharing between regulatory sandbox participants is recommended, such as a chatroom. Finally, a regulatory sandbox manual is recommended to be created to provide clear guidance and instructions on the regulatory sandbox's procedures, policies, scope and objectives. This manual can help streamline the application process and ensure that participants are aware of their obligations and responsibilities while participating in the regulatory sandbox.

Figure 2.8. Means of the communication strategy

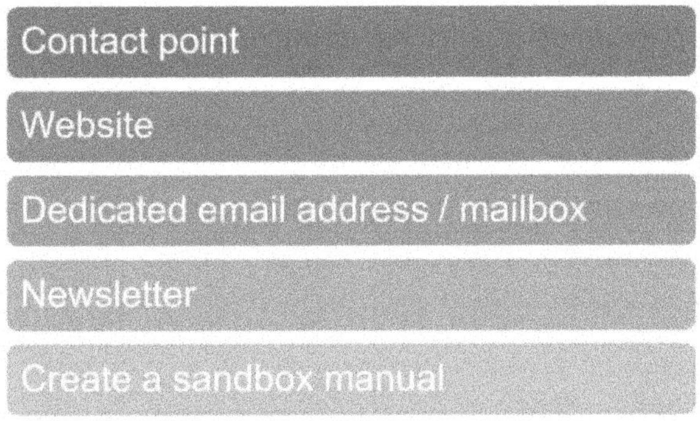

For FinTech companies, the communication strategy should provide clear and consistent information on the regulatory sandbox's goals, requirements, processes and limits (in particular that no exemptions or waivers are provided). Regular updates on the status of their application and clear instructions on how to participate in the regulatory sandbox should be communicated. Ensuring this helps to minimise confusion and guarantees that the FinTech companies are equipped with the information they need to be successful in the regulatory sandbox.

The communication strategy should also include the means by which the relevant regulators, those that have responsibilities concerning financial service providers (see OECD (2022[13])), will communicate with each other and with other stakeholders such as industry associations and consumer groups, for example to inform them of participating firms or of exit of firms from the testing phase, or if any issues concerning consumer protection and a participating firm have arisen. It is generally agreed that a website (regularly maintained) is a suitable strategy. This will ensure that all parties are aware of any updates or changes to the requirements of the regulatory sandbox, timelines, forms etc.

In the third place, the communication strategy should consider the ways in which the results of the regulatory sandbox will be communicated to the wider public. This may include regular reports on the progress of the regulatory sandbox and its impact on the FinTech industry, as well as highlighting success stories and best practices.

When designing the communication strategy for a regulatory sandbox for FinTechs in the Czech Republic, it is important to consider ways to reduce the application and evaluation process time. This can be achieved by expanding communication channels and encouraging participants to discuss their applications through various means such as email, video conferencing, face to face meetings, or establishing direct contact with specific divisions' representatives. However, such facilitating measures during the application phase could not be made available by the CNB, which currently cannot commit to provide this capacity. In addition to this, efforts should be made to simplify and reduce the paperwork involved in the application and inspection process. To facilitate this, the creation of a dedicated website can be considered. The website can provide clear and concise information on the application process, evaluation criteria, and contact information for relevant departments. This would not only reduce the administrative burden on applicants but also provide a central location for stakeholders to access information and keep up-to-date with the latest developments.

Occasionally, entrepreneurs lack the necessary legal expertise to understand how the financial operations or new product they intend to develop are regulated and supervised. In this situation, the relevant authority should strongly consider devoting additional capacity to advising and communicating due to the absence of a thorough grasp of financial legislation (APEC Economic Committee, 2021[25]).

The objectives of the communication strategy are illustrated in Figure 2.9. A clear and effective communication strategy can help build trust and confidence in the regulatory sandbox, encourage participation and promote the benefits of innovation in the financial sector. The communication strategy serves to inform and engage different stakeholders in the regulatory sandbox, including FinTech companies, investors, regulators, and the general public. For FinTech companies, the communication strategy should focus on providing clear and transparent information on the paperwork, application, entrance, and exit requirements. For other stakeholders, the strategy should highlight the purpose, advances, and challenges of the regulatory sandbox, including the potential impact on the financial industry. The general public should be informed of the purpose and expected impacts of the regulatory sandbox, as well as the measures in place to protect consumers.

Figure 2.9. Objectives of the communication strategy

Relevant authorities should comprehensively explain basic characteristics of the regulatory sandbox on their website and other communication channels and link to the web page of the regulatory sandbox, promote the information of the establishment of the regulatory sandbox and share excerpts from public updates on regulatory sandbox activities prepared by the Czech Authorities. It is recommended that participants should sufficiently familiarise themselves with regulatory sandbox rules prior to applying for participation in the sandbox. Participants should also actively engage with the Czech Authorities and respond timely in order to use the testing phase efficiently.

2.5. Action plan for the implementation of the regulatory sandbox

Table 2.6. Proposed timeline for the implementation of a regulatory sandbox

	Task	Actor	Timeline
1	Pre-application Phase	3-5 months	
	Communication strategy: set up the various layers of communication regarding the regulatory sandbox including establishing a dedicated website and email address, a regulatory sandbox manual, and various additional tools	Czech Authorities	30-45 days
	Application portal: develop an application portal consistent with all criteria to be reviewed initially by the Advisory Board and later validated by the Authorities	Czech Authorities	30-45 days
	Establish the Advisory Board: set up an Advisory Board for applicant pre-selection comprising of representatives of industry, academia, relevant ministries and authorities	Czech Authorities	30-60 days

	Task	Actor	Timeline
2	Application Phase	Ongoing	
	Publicly launch regulatory sandbox: launch elements of the communication plan and announce application portal opening with regular updating of the communication materials	Czech Authorities	1-2 days of launch
	Application assessment by Advisory Board: the application portal is recommended to be continuously open, and applications are to be gathered by the Advisory Board every 90 days (max.)	Advisory Board	≤ 90 days
3	Review Phase	≤ 3 months	
	Application review by Advisory Board and the Czech Authorities: applicants are to be preselected by the Advisory Board and validated or rejected by the Czech Authorities in 90 days intervals (max.)	Advisory Board, the Czech Authorities	≤ 90 days
	Deliver outcome to applicants: applicants will be notified whether their application is successful, incomplete, or rejected	Czech Authorities	1-2 days post review
	Contact successful applicants: successful applicants are to be contacted and made aware of next steps and assigned to the relevant contact person	Czech Authorities	1-2 days post acceptance
4	Testing Phase	13 months	
	Preparation of testing plan: over the following 60 days, the successful applicant together with the contact person prepare a testing plan that the sandbox participant must comply with. If the company is not already licensed and during the construction of the testing plan the Czech Authorities advises the company to apply for a specific license, this stage, including the licensing procedure will be determined by the administrative rules.	Czech Authorities, CNB	60 days, or until license is granted
	Assess proposed testing plan: the testing plan is to be reviewed by the Authorities	Czech Authorities	on a case-by-case
	Implement testing plan: implementation logistics will vary on a case-by-case basis and testing timelines are proposed to be 12 months	Czech Authorities	12 months
	Conduct checkpoint meetings and reviews: the participant and the contact point are to be in regular contact on the progress of the testing environment	Czech Authorities	Ongoing
5	Exit and Review	3 months	
	Approve exit in case of early termination: the exit plan produced in the application phase will be reviewed by the Authorities in case early termination is requested	Czech Authorities	30 days
	Review and discussion of exit report submitted by the firm: the firm is to produce a report analysing the results of the regulatory sandbox testing experience	Czech Authorities	30 days
	Collect and document lessons learned: lessons learned from the sandbox experience can be gathered through interviews of participants, analysis of reports, etc	Czech Authorities	30 days

References

APEC Economic Committee (2021), "FinTech Regulatory Sandboxes Capacity Building Summary Report", *Asia-Pacific Economic Cooperation Secretariat*, http://www.cbr.ru (accessed on 20 March 2023). [25]

APIX (2023), *Sandbox | Collaborative Integrated Development Environment (IDE)*, APIX, https://apixplatform.com/sandbox (accessed on 11 May 2023). [4]

Banco de España (2022), *Controlled testing space (sandbox)*, Banco de España, https://www.bde.es/wbe/en/entidades-profesionales/operativa-gestiones/autorizaciones-acreditaciones/facilitadores-innovacion/espacio-controlado-pruebas-sandbox.html (accessed on 5 May 2023). [10]

Bromberg, L., A. Godwin and I. Ramsay (2017), "Fintech sandboxes: Achieving a balance between regulation and innovation", *Journal of Banking and Finance Law and Practice*, Vol. 28/4, pp. 314-336. [16]

Czech National Bank (n.d.), *Uplatňování individuálních diskrecí orgánem dohledu*, https://www.cnb.cz/cs/legislativa/vykon-cinnosti-a-obezretnostni-pravidla/uplatnovani-individualnich-diskreci-organem-dohledu/ (accessed on 29 March 2023). [12]

Deloitte (2017), *Regulatory Sandbox - Making India a Global Fintech Hub*. [6]

Dirección General de Estabilidad Financiera, I. et al. (2022), *Synthetic data pilot with Banco de España, Findings and recommendations*, FISMA, https://www.cde.ual.es/ficha/synthetic-data-pilot-with-banco-de-espana-findings-and-recommendations/ (accessed on 5 May 2023). [18]

EBA (2021), *Final Report on Guidelines on internal governance under Directive 2013/36/EU*, EBA, https://www.eba.europa.eu/sites/default/documents/files/document_library/Publications/Guidelines/2021/1016721/Final%20report%20on%20Guidelines%20on%20internal%20governance%20under%20CRD.pdf (accessed on 29 March 2023). [11]

EBRD (2019), *Poland: Feasibility study on innovative technological solutions in the Polish financial markets including building a Regulatory Sandbox*, ERBD, https://www.ebrd.com/work-with-us/projects/tcpsd/poland-feasibility-study-on-innovative-technological-solutions-in-the-polish-financial-markets-including-building-a-regulatory-sandbox.html (accessed on 2 May 2023). [7]

ESMA, EBA and EIOPA (2019), *FinTech: Regulatory sandboxes and innovation hubs*, https://ec.europa.eu/info/publications/180308-action-plan-fintech_en. (accessed on 5 May 2023). [2]

ESMA, EBA and EIOPA (2018), *FinTech: Regulatory sandboxes and innovation hubs*, https://ec.europa.eu/info/publications/180308-action-plan-fintech_en. (accessed on 29 August 2022). [8]

European Commission (2020), *Technology readiness levels (TRL)*, https://ec.europa.eu/research/participants/data/ref/h2020/wp/2014_2015/annexes/h2020-wp1415-annex-g-trl_en.pdf (accessed on 11 May 2023). [21]

FCA (2021), *Supporting innovation in financial services: the digital sandbox pilot*, https://www.fca.org.uk/publication/corporate/digital-sandbox-joint-report.pdf (accessed on 20 March 2023). [17]

FCA (2017), *Regulatory sandbox lessons learned report*, FCA, https://www.fca.org.uk/publication/research-and-data/regulatory-sandbox-lessons-learned-report.pdf (accessed on 5 May 2023). [22]

FCA (2015), *Regulatory sandbox*, FCA. [15]

Government of Singapore (2022), *Monetary Authority of Singapore (MAS) APIs - Streamlining of Financial Applications through Data | Singapore Government Developer Portal*, Government of Singapore, https://www.developer.tech.gov.sg/products/categories/data-and-apis/mas-apis/overview.html (accessed on 11 May 2023). [3]

Hořínek, D. (2022), *CzechInvest seeks innovative startups for Technology Incubation*, CzechInvest, https://www.czechinvest.org/en/Homepage/News/June-2022/CzechInvest-seeks-innovative-startups-for-Technology-Incubation (accessed on 29 March 2023). [14]

Israel Innovation Authority (n.d.), *How to evaluate routes in the growth division*, https://innovationisrael.org.il/general_content/3813 (accessed on 11 May 2023). [20]

Jenik, I. and K. Lauer (2017), "Regulatory sandboxes and financial inclusion", *cgap.org*, https://www.cgap.org/sites/default/files/researches/documents/Working-Paper-Regulatory-Sandboxes-Oct-2017.pdf (accessed on 19 April 2022). [19]

OECD (2022), *The FinTech Ecosystem in the Czech Republic*, OECD Publishing, Paris, https://doi.org/10.1787/068ba90e-en. [13]

OECD/Eurostat (2018), *Oslo Manual 2018: Guidelines for Collecting, Reporting and Using Data on Innovation, 4th Edition*, The Measurement of Scientific, Technological and Innovation Activities, OECD Publishing, Paris/Eurostat, Luxembourg, https://doi.org/10.1787/9789264304604-en. [1]

Parenti, R. (2020), "Regulatory sandboxes and innovation hubs for FinTech", *Study for the committee on Economic and Monetary Affairs, Policy Department for Economic, Scientific and Quality of Life Policies, European Parliament, Luxembourg,* September. [9]

The Bank of Lithuania (2018), *RESOLUTION ON THE APPROVAL OF THE REGULATORY SANDBOX FRAMEWORK OF THE BANK OF LITHUANIA*, Bank of Lithuania, https://www.lb.lt/uploads/documents/files/EN/our-functions/supervision-of-financial-institutions/sandbox/03-166_2018%2009%2019_EN.pdf (accessed on 29 March 2023). [23]

The Ministry of Information Technologies and Communications (2023), *Datos Abiertos Colombia*, https://www.datos.gov.co/en/ (accessed on 11 May 2023). [5]

World Bank (2020), *How Regulators Respond to Fintech: Evaluating the Different Approaches-Sandboxes and Beyond*, World Bank. [24]

Notes

[1] British FCA is establishing a Synthetic Data Expert Group. Source: Synthetic Data Call for Input Feedback Statement, pg. 9

[2] Technically speaking, the creation of synthetics that are entirely artificial is possible, however, the relevance compared to the real data is expected to be inexistent if not based on existing datasets.

[3] digital-finance-platform.ec.europa.eu

[4] This means the following categories of firms can participate: companies that already have a license within the financial legislation, but wish to test a new technology and/or business model; companies that do not have the required license within the financial legislation to provide the desired activity; companies where it is uncertain whether the activity requires a license within the financial legislation.

[5] e.g. Act No. 21/1992 Coll., on Banks, as amended, Act No. 240/2013 Coll., on Management Companies and. Investment Funds, as amended, Act No. 256/2004 Coll., on Capital Market Business, as amended, and Act No. 190/2004 Coll., on Bonds, as amended.

[6] Article 32 of Directive (EU) 2015/2366 of the European Parliament and of the Council of 25 November 2015 on payment services in the internal market, amending Directives 2002/65/EC, 2009/110/EC and 2013/36/EU and Regulation (EU) No 1093/2010, and repealing Directive 2007/64/EC https://eur-lex.europa.eu/legal-content/EN/TXT/?uri=CELEX%3A02015L2366-2015 1223

[7] Section 58 (2) "A small-scale payment service provider is authorised to provide payment services only if the monthly average of the amounts of payment transactions executed by this provider in the Czech Republic, including payment transactions executed through its authorised agents, does not exceed the amount of EUR 3, 000, 000 for the last 12 months. If a small-scale payment service provider is a member of a group, these average monthly amounts also include payment transactions that the other small-scale payment service providers, which are members of the group, have executed in the Czech Republic over the last 12 months, including payment transactions made through their authorised agents."

[8] C-18/14 – CO Sociedad de Gestion y Participación and Others https://curia.europa.eu/juris/liste.jsf?num=C-18/14

[9] Consolidated text: Directive 2013/36/EU of the European Parliament and of the Council of 26 June 2013 on access to the activity of credit institutions and the prudential supervision of credit institutions, amending Directive 2002/87/EC and repealing Directives 2006/48/EC and 2006/49/EC https://eur-lex.europa.eu/legal-content/EN/TXT/?uri=CELEX%3A02013L0036-20220101

[10] Regulation (EU) No 575/2013 of the European Parliament and of the Council of 26 June 2013 on prudential requirements for credit institutions and investment firms and amending Regulation (EU) No 648/2012 https://eur-lex.europa.eu/legal-content/EN/TXT/?uri=celex%3A32013R0575

[11] See more on the mandate of the CNB in the Annex.

[12] The only reference among reviewed jurisdictions where the team was able to find regarding the level of Technology Readiness Level (TRL) is the Israeli pilot in FinTech regime, where the eligibility criteria mention a TRL of 6-8. https://innovationisrael.org.il/general_content/3813

Annex A. Background to the feasibility report and lessons learned

This section provides context behind the in-depth feasibility study performed on the FinTech ecosystem in the Czech Republic, of which the main findings are presented in Chapter 1, which formed the basis of the recommendations presented in this report for the implementation of a regulatory sandbox presented in Chapter 2. The purpose, objectives, activities, and all relevant details regarding the execution of the feasibility study for a regulatory sandbox in the Czech Republic are presented here, as per the Action underpinning this project.

Purpose and objectives of the feasibility study for a regulatory sandbox in the Czech Republic

The mission of the Directorate General for Structural Reform Support (DG REFORM) of the European Commission is to promote the European Union's economic, social and territorial cohesion by supporting Member States' efforts to implement reforms. The Czech Republic has requested support from the European Commission under Regulation (EU) 2021/240 establishing a Technical Support Instrument ("TSI Regulation"). Following the assessment, the European Commission has decided to fund the request and provide technical support to the Czech Republic, together with the Organisation for Economic Co-operation and Development (OECD). The technical support was provided in the area of administrative and regulatory reform, with the purpose of establishing a regulatory sandbox for Financial Technology (FinTech)[1] companies in the Czech Republic.

FinTech can improve the efficiency of the financial sector, all the more so in the context of the digitalisation trend that was intensified during the COVID-19 pandemic. However, modern technologies and the advantages of the Czech IT sector (technical capacities, skills) are not used to their full potential, and there is no innovation facilitator dedicated to FinTechs in the Czech Republic. Importantly, the level of innovation and technical complexity of FinTech applications lead to perceived uncertainty about the existence and/or applicability of relevant regulatory and supervisory frameworks.

The objectives of the Action were to analyse the current and potential use of data in finance and related policy frameworks and to support the growth of FinTech in the Czech Republic by providing recommendations on the design of a regulatory sandbox with a dedicated testing data-sharing and data usage infrastructure to harness the potential of FinTech innovation while limiting emerging risks and safeguarding the financial system.

Activities and outputs outlined in the action

In order to achieve the objectives of the Action, The OECD has implemented the Action in a gradual manner, producing several intermediate reports (Figure A A.1), through continuous consultation with relevant Czech stakeholders and several workshops dedicated to presenting best practices and findings related to the Czech ecosystem, spur a discussion and receive feedback.

Figure A A.1. Project outputs

The Action was launched with a **kick-off event** that took place on 5 May 2022, in Prague, with attendees representing all stakeholder groups concerned by the Action. In parallel, the OECD team initiated an outreach effort towards many relevant stakeholders, with requests for physical meetings/interviews and tailored questionnaires. Extensive consultations took place with the Czech National Bank, the Czech Ministry of Finance and Czech FinTech organisations. Several other stakeholders have provided the team with written answers to questions. With a focus on start-ups and SMEs, the OECD published an online questionnaire, focusing on the following issues: people and skills; corporate finance; innovation and data management; compliance and risk. An **inception report** was submitted to DG REFORM on 1 July 2022 and presented the operational aspects of the Action including the organisational structure; description of activities; timeline; information needs; methodology; communication arrangements; external communication plans; feedback processes and potential risks associated with the implementation of the Action.

On 20 September 2022 the OECD organised a webinar where it presented the preliminary findings of the **Czech FinTech sector and ecosystem mapping** and received feedback from participants. Given that there was no comprehensive country study describing the FinTech sector of the Czech Republic, the mapping report was published as an OECD report to improve visibility of the Action and provide a solid basis for local and international stakeholders (including investors). It was submitted to DG REFORM on the 14th of October 2022 and publicly launched at an event on 24th of November 2022 in Prague.

The **mapping report** reviewed the current regulatory and supervisory framework in terms of (i) different types of licenses and authorisations, (ii) the relevant processes, and (iii) the involved stakeholders. An assessment of the potential impact of the new EU legislative proposals on the local FinTech market has also been done. This assessment was based on thorough analysis of the implications expected at the current proposed regulatory framework compared with the existing supervisory and regulatory framework.

The report assessed that there were more than 100 the Czech FinTech companies operating in the Czech Republic at the time, active across a number of regulated and unregulated sectors of activity. Financial market activity in the Czech Republic is regulated by the Ministry of Finance of the Czech Republic (MFCR) which develops and enacts the financial market policy and drafts legislation. The Czech National Bank (CNB) is the sole unified supervisory authority for the financial markets in the country. In November 2019, the CNB established a FinTech contact point. The contact point aims at helping resolve unclear regulatory issues – including licensing and supervisory ones – so as to facilitate compliance with the duties applied to market participants by financial market regulations. Opinions of the CNB provided via the contact point do not substitute for authorisations or approvals granted in licensing proceedings and are not binding in any way. EU legislation proposals under way are expected to bring more entities into the regulatory scope, to achieve a harmonised legal framework across the EU. This will ultimately increase the number of entities that the CNB will need to authorise and supervise.

Twenty-four FinTech companies provided detailed responses to the online questionnaire as of 5 October 2022, representing almost a quarter of the Czech FinTech companies' universe. Access to data is critical for FinTechs and data is at the core of most FinTech activity (e.g. artificial intelligence business models in trading; lending; blockchain-based solutions in finance). Indeed, more than 67% of respondents to the OECD Questionnaire stated that access to both financial and non-financial data is beneficial to their business development. When it comes to data sharing secured by formal regulatory arrangements and frameworks, such as PSD 2, data accessibility is not guaranteed. More than 46% of firms responding to the OECD Questionnaire have had problems accessing customer data from financial intermediaries.

According to the findings of the OECD Questionnaire, the most important reported hurdles to FinTech innovations in the Czech Republic are related to regulation: lack of regulatory clarity (67%), red tape (63%), licensing and supervisory requirements (58%), followed by entry barriers (54% of respondents). According to the OECD survey, 71% of respondent FinTechs would be interested in taking part in a sandbox with a focus on data, if it were to become available. Two-thirds of these would only be interested in participating depending on the terms of such a sandbox. The answers highlighted the importance of a well-thought design and structure of any future sandbox arrangement, and also a possible lack of clear understanding of what a sandbox involves from the FinTech side, underlining the importance of clear communication and the required educational effort that may need to be undertaken ahead of a possible future establishment of a sandbox.

The 2nd Workshop of the Action was held on 24th of November at the Czech Republic Ministry of Finance in Prague. The Workshop gathered 62 participants from the public sector, the private sector including FinTechs and associations representing the industry, academia and other local and international authorities' representatives. A preliminary analysis on gaps was presented and an open discussion with participants from all parts of the ecosystem around the identified gaps and the alternative policies to fill in gaps and alleviate constraints to the development of the Czech FinTech ecosystem was held. The workshop also included knowledge sharing session on data sharing arrangements, and a roundtable discussion on the Czech FinTech ecosystem.

The **feasibility report**, submitted to DG REFORM in January 2023, highlights best practices in policy frameworks across OECD economies in order to support the development of FinTech. With these best practices in mind, the report then analyses the current regulatory and supervisory framework implemented in the Czech Republic and documents gaps and barriers related to other aspects of the Czech financial markets that may hinder the development of the Czech FinTech sector. The report highlights financial literacy and capital market development as areas where improvements are needed in the Czech Republic in order to align with best practices. There are indications that the current dialogue between the CNB and FinTechs may not be optimal. This is why the report recommends the establishment of a form of innovation facilitator, as a way to promote the diffusion of understanding and knowledge of regulations, supervision, and norms, while at the same time informing the authorities of the impacts of regulations, thus not only driving innovation in the market, but also within the authorities.

In particular, an innovation facilitator, such as a regulatory sandbox, could reinforce the limited capacity of the FinTech contact point, especially in light of forthcoming changes to the FinTech-related regulatory environment and the associated higher needs for guidance by FinTechs. The final report **develops specific recommendations** as a result of the analysis, in close consultation with the Czech National Bank and the Ministry of Finance, on the design of a sandbox for the Czech Republic. These recommendations draw on experience of sandbox models in other jurisdictions and are adjusted to cater for the specific needs of the Czech financial ecosystem.

The recommendation for the Czech sandbox is to commence with the establishment of a 'standard' sandbox, fully managed by the Czech Authorities, and to the extent feasible, provide data-sharing when the conditions allow it. The feasibility of this option will be based on (i) availability of datasets and ability to make these available; (ii) capacity of the authorities participating in the sandbox. The recommended scope for the Czech sandbox would be firms offering an innovative product or service, with no restrictions as to the sector of activity, provided that these fall under the remit of the financial supervisor (CNB) directly or indirectly. Therefore, any financial activity could be considered for participation in the Czech sandbox, provided that applicant firms comply with eligibility criteria provided. The recommended structure for the Czech sandbox advises against the provision of any waivers; restricted authorisations or other relaxation of existing applicable rules, which would anyway be against EU rules. It is recommended that a proportional application of existing regulatory and supervisory requirements, as embedded in EU financial services regulation, is used as appropriate and at the discretion of the supervisor for firms participating in the Czech sandbox. The sandbox should offer firms individual guidance and attractive timelines for the various phases of the test.

Lessons learned during the implementation of the Action

Importance of building communication channels between different stakeholders in the FinTech ecosystem

Effective communication between all stakeholders involved in the FinTech ecosystem is of paramount importance for the development of the FinTech market. Without functioning and collaborative communication channels in place, it is difficult to advance and foster the FinTech market, as differing standpoints and perceptions may not be known or well-understood by stakeholders involved. In the case of the Czech FinTech ecosystem, FinTechs perceived the CNB as siding with the large incumbent institutions and lacking the intention to help foster the business environment for FinTechs and promote their growth. The CNB, on the other hand, may not have fully reaped the benefits of interacting with FinTech firms to promote its understanding of their business models or to address the perceived impediments to their growth.

Communication gaps between the CNB and FinTechs caused issues in the payments service provider licensing process. An example of a hurdle encountered by FinTech firms in the area of Payment Service Providers is obtaining a license. The CNB has been facing elevated demand for licensing authorisations by various payment entities since the implementation of PSD2 regulatory framework, while at the same time expressing dissatisfaction with the quality of such applications. Approval ratios for these entities are low and the number of payments services providers has been declining since 2018 due to stricter requirements of the new PSD2 rules, as well as CNB's enforcement of them and of AML requirements.

A regulatory sandbox can improve dialogue and reduce burdens encountered or perceived by the FinTech industry. To have a deeper understanding of the main hurdles that FinTechs are encountered with, the OECD conducted a questionnaire to gather insights from an industry perspective. The main reported issues were primarily around regulation; the lack of regulatory clarity, red tape, and licensing requirements being on the top of the list. The findings indicate that there indeed is reason for improving the communication channels between the supervisor and FinTechs, and a regulatory sandbox could be one of the ways to improve dialogue and alleviate some of the reported burdens encountered by this sector, with benefits for both authorities and FinTechs.

A form of innovation facilitator set up by the authorities could have an important signalling effect

There are conflicting perceptions between FinTech firms and regulators/supervisor. Related to the issue of lack of communication, there seems to be clashing perceptions between FinTech firms and regulators/supervisor. Authorities on the one hand may somehow perceive many FinTechs as endeavours that are unwilling or unable to invest into understanding and ensuring compliance with existing rules (which they label as "red tape") and wish to remain outside the scope of the regulator for regulatory arbitrage purposes. FinTechs on the other hand seem to perceive regulators and supervisors as unwilling to provide guidance or help the development of the FinTech industry, despite the potential of these firms to produce possible efficiencies and other benefits towards society at large. Such generalised perceptions are counter-productive and do not reflect the reality of the situation since regulation and oversight provides for shared benefits and strives for common objectives between FinTechs and authorities, such as safeguarding consumer protection which will increase the confidence of consumers in innovative services.

A regulatory sandbox could serve as an important signalling tool used by authorities to demonstrate their willingness to foster safe and resilient development of the FinTech industry. From a signalling perspective, the regulatory sandbox could still extend benefits to the FinTech ecosystem irrespective of whether the sandbox is big or small in scale and contains few or multiple features. The initiative could signal the effort made by authorities in attempting to promote a better dialogue with FinTechs firms and foster the development of a safe FinTech ecosystem. It could therefore ameliorate the current perception held by many in the FinTech industry about a possible negative stance that regulatory and supervisory bodies take towards innovation within the financial sector. In parallel, it is important to allocate the appropriate capacity and offer real measurable benefits to sandbox participants, such as customary guidelines and attractive timelines, alongside a true intention to support innovation, to improve the current perception.

There is a lack of education of FinTechs on the role and need for regulation in safeguarding themselves, their customers, and the financial markets

Many Czech FinTechs, especially the young start-ups among them, lack understanding of the important role that regulation plays in the safeguarding of their own activities, the financial consumers that form the base of their customers, and the financial markets within which they operate. Many of the FinTechs that were consulted during the exploration and analysis phases of the project lacked a solid understanding around the fundamental objectives of regulation in the financial markets and of the specifics of regulatory and supervisory requirements of financial activity. While this is not uncommon for many FinTech firms in advanced economies, there is a possible need for increased financial education efforts towards FinTechs (and micro, small and medium enterprises MSMEs more broadly).

Increased financial education towards FinTechs may be needed. The possible establishment of an innovation facilitator in the form of a regulatory sandbox could also contribute to such efforts as a positive by-product given the close collaboration of the supervisor with participating firms.

Note

[1] According to the Financial Stability Board (FSB), Financial Technology (FinTech) can be defined as "*technology-enabled innovation in financial services that could result in new business models, applications, processes or products and could have an associated material effect on financial markets and institutions and how financial services are provided*".

Annex B. Background to innovation facilitators

In order to better understand new FinTech activities, business models, hazards, and motivations, the numerous platforms for regulatory outreach to the FinTech industry have become increasingly institutionalised through "innovation facilitators" that have taken different forms, depending on the jurisdiction, and mostly taking the form of innovation hubs and/or sandboxes. As it has been recommended in a number of OECD jurisdictions, including the European Union (EU) and the United States, it is important to consider the integration of specific entity-based regulations to address the emerging policy problems (Carstens et al., 2021[1]). Each jurisdiction has a distinct FinTech flavour which is influenced by these initiatives and the larger regulatory environment, and regulatory sandboxes have already become mainstream (Ahern et al., 2023[2]).

Innovation facilitators share the objective of supporting the potential of FinTech innovation while at the same time limiting risks and safeguarding the financial system. Innovation facilitators provide customised guidance to firms and intend to promote an active and constructive dialogue that benefits all stakeholders in the FinTech ecosystem. Furthermore, innovation facilitators promote the diffusion of understanding and knowledge of regulations, supervisions and norms, while at the same time informing the regulatory and supervisory authorities of the impacts of regulations, thus not only driving innovation in the market but also within the regulatory and supervisory bodies. Innovation facilitators can also enhance legal certainty: rules and regulations continue to apply; there is no bending of the rules for FinTechs.

EU national innovation facilitators are brought together by the European Forum on Innovation Facilitators (EFIF).[1] EFIF shares experiences from engagement with firms through sandboxes and innovation hubs, exchanges technological expertise, and seeks to reach consensus on the regulatory treatment of innovative products and services, along with producing case studies (such as RegTech) and cross-border testing. All 27 EU Member States (in the securities, banking, and insurance sectors) as well as three European Economic Area (EEA) countries (Iceland, Liechtenstein and Norway) are members of the EFIF. Both regulators and innovators recognise the benefits of innovation hubs and regulatory sandboxes. These benefits include spurring innovation while staying alert to emerging risks, reduced asymmetric information, and reduced regulatory costs or uncertainty (ESMA, EBA and EIOPA, 2019[3]). Additionally, authorities have observed increased engagement with FinTech firms as a result of these facilitators.[2]

An innovation hub is a facilitator of innovation that has been established by a supervisory body to assist enterprises, whether regulated or not, in navigating the regulatory landscape or in identifying supervisory policy or legal issues and concerns. Innovation hubs have usually a central point of contact for FinTechs to communicate directly with the authorities and get clarity on compliance with licencing standards and/or regulatory frameworks. FinTechs can benefit from innovation hubs to navigate the legal, policy, and regulatory systems. The support provided might be direct or indirect, through market direction, and often excludes product or service testing (World Bank, 2020[4]). Germany and the Bank for International Settlements (BIS) have established such innovation hubs for FinTech support.[3]

References

Ahern, D. et al. (2023), "The Role of Sectoral Regulators and other State Actors in Formulating Novel and Alternative Pro-Competition Mechanisms In Fintech", http://www.tara.tcd.ie/handle/2262/101 066 (accessed on 19 December 2022). [2]

Carstens, A. et al. (2021), *Regulating big techs in finance*, BIS Bulletin No 45, http://www.bis.org (accessed on 19 December 2022). [1]

ESMA, EBA and EIOPA (2019), *FinTech: Regulatory sandboxes and innovation hubs*, https://ec.europa.eu/info/publications/180308-action-plan-fintech_en. (accessed on 5 May 2023). [3]

World Bank (2020), "Global Experiences from Regulatory Sandboxes", *Fintech* Note, No. 8, World Bank, Washington DC, https://doi.org/10.1596/34789. [4]

Notes

[1] The EFIF is run jointly by the European Securities and Markets Authority (ESMA), the European Banking Authority (EBA), and the European Insurance and Occupational Pensions Authority (EIOPA) in collaboration with the European Commission (DG FISMA).

[2] Presentation delivered at the OECD Workshop in Prague on 24 November 2022.

[3] Presentation delivered at the OECD Workshop in Prague on 24 November 2022.

Annex C. Practical examples of data sandboxes

Spain

Banco de España participated in the synthetic data pilot led by the European Commission with the aim of supporting the creation of the future EU Digital Finance Platform's Data Hub. The pilot consisted of testing the procedure of generating synthetic data on the Central Balance Sheet (CBI) and Loans to Legal Entities (CIR) datasets available in the Banco de España's (BELab) data laboratory. The initial results obtained during the pilot were overall positive and encouraging for further exploration of the technology. However, some limitations were identified in the data such as suppression of outliers, imbalances among variables, and the impossibility of merging synthetic datasets.

The pilot highlighted that synthetising data should be considered as a cross-sectional project requiring collaboration from multiple departments within the supervisor and commitment from the software provider. Although BELab shortened the time needed to synthetise the data, the process was highly time and resource-consuming and required highly specialised staff.

Banco de España believes that synthetic data could be a valuable contribution to the sandboxes and cross-border testing, but the limitations detected in the data may hinder its use in certain cases. Therefore, market participants should be aware of these limitations. The results of the pilot should not be taken as the sole source of information when specifying the conditions of the tender or building the future data hub. Further analysis and more time are needed to obtain more reliable conclusions.

United Kingdom

The Financial Conduct Authority (FCA), together with the City of London Corporation, has successfully established a digital sandbox, with two pilot projects already underway offering access to synthetic data sets for testing and PoC development. The first pilot project ran from October 2020 to February 2021 and focused on improving SME finance, detecting and preventing fraud and supporting the financial resilience of vulnerable customers. The second pilot ran from October 2021 to March 2022 and focused on financial innovation linked to sustainability. In addition to synthetic data sets, the pilots offered participants access to a range of other development tools, such as APIs, programming environments, as well as access to expert mentors and observers.

The synthetic data was the most valuable feature cited by participants while simultaneously the one with greatest potential for improvement. Notably, referentially linked data sets and more granular data would enable more effective testing, and for products to be developed further. Overall, 84% of responders cited the pilot as having accelerated their product development. While it is difficult to ascertain or quantify this level of acceleration, analysis shows that the biggest factor was ready access to data in developing an early stage PoC. Several participants estimated they had accelerated their development by 4-6 months, with one going as high as 18-24 months, largely by negating the initial need to identify and work with an industry partner to get a PoC off the ground, or sourcing or generating data themselves.

Those who found that the pilot tools had not accelerated or improved their development generally noted that this related to the data being insufficient in some way for meeting their use case. This was as a result of one or a combination of the following:

Insufficient detail in the data, particularly a lack of relevant typologies or behaviours they required to model their solutions. For example, transactional spending patterns indicative of a customer experiencing fluctuating mental health (under the vulnerable consumers use cases) were not seeded into the synthetic data due to the complexity of doing so.

Required data sets were not available. For example, large volumes of unstructured data such as consumer complaints text, to train and validate natural language processing techniques.

Data sets not being referentially linked. For example, different data sets had been generated independently, so the behavioural patterns or characteristics of a synthetic individual 'John Smith', would not be consistent with 'John Smith' in a separate data set.

However, even with these limitations, participants noted the utility of the data sets for 'bootstrapping' product design. Even where the data could not be used to refine an algorithmic model, there was value in providing the data models, data structures and formats that were representative of what they would be working with in real production environments (FCA, 2021[1]).

It should also be noted that in the United Kingdom, the process of developing FinTech solutions has been optimised through years of experience and innovation in the sector. A systematic approach has been established, starting with the definition of a problem and letting FinTech companies explore possible solutions. The next step is a Tech Sprint, which involves defining the problem and providing datasets to develop proof of concept (PoC). The Digital Sandbox phase builds on the PoC, further testing the potential solutions and their viability. Finally, the Regulatory Sandbox assesses the regulatory requirements for the minimum viable product (MVP) developed during the previous stages. This step-by-step process provides a clear path for the development and implementation of innovative FinTech solutions, allowing for a seamless transition from concept to market-ready product (Figure A C.1).

Figure A C.1. Digital and regulatory sandboxes based on the systematic approach of the UK FCA

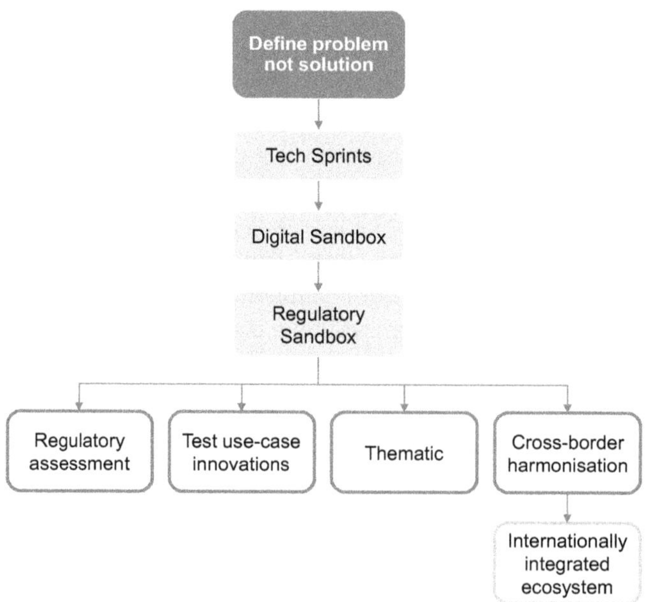

There are several countries that have implemented data sandboxes, including Australia, Singapore, the United Kingdom, and Canada. However, the only sandbox targeted at financial innovation that has offered participants access to financial data thus far has been the FCA, with the last two cohorts offering a data attribute.

Australia

The Australian Competition and Consumer Commission (ACCC) has established a consumer data right (CDR) Sandbox[1] to support the development and testing of CDR-related solutions by businesses. The Competition and Consumer Commission (ACCC) has created a "mock" registry, "mock" data holder, and "mock" data recipient CDR repository to help businesses develop and test CDR solutions within their own IT environment. This mock environment has been downloaded more than 20 000 times from GitHub and has received positive feedback from CDR participants and platform providers. The ACCC is now launching a hosted sandbox environment to build upon these mock tools, allowing businesses to test CDR solutions with other participants and to validate technical solutions early in the software development cycle. This sandbox has the potential to lower the barrier for businesses to join the CDR and increase the quality of solutions. The ACCC anticipates the sandbox will be broadly adopted by CDR participants and enable common platforms to be tested against other systems prior to widespread implementation.

References

FCA (2021), *Supporting innovation in financial services: the digital sandbox pilot*, https://www.fca.org.uk/publication/corporate/digital-sandbox-joint-report.pdf (accessed on 20 March 2023). [1]

Note

[1]Australia lists the type of data available for the sandbox through the following link: https://github.com/ConsumerDataRight/sandbox.

Annex D. Examples of regulatory sandboxes

Table A D.1. Austrian sandbox

No.	Area	
1.	Institution(s) involved in the selection of participants and the operation of the regulatory sandbox	Financial Market Authority. The establishment and operation of the regulatory sandbox was achieved by means of legislative amendment in the underlying legal framework of the FMA to allow for the establishment and operation of the sandbox under its competence. Article 23a of the Financial Market Authority Act (FMABG; Finanzmarktaufsichtsbehördengesetz) entered into force on 01 September 2020. It provides the FMA with the necessary competence for and establishes the framework for the sandbox. The FMA is only allowed to act on the basis of this law, and not allowed to use free discretion to decide about a participant in the regulatory sandbox.
		FMA informs Federal Minister of Finance about applications. An advisory board (Regulatory Sandbox Beirat) established at the Federal Ministry of Finance for assessing the impact of sandbox business models, the rules of procedure of which shall be defined by the Federal Minister of Finance.
		The Regulatory Sandbox Beirat shall submit an opinion to the FMA about the existence of the economic interest pursuant to para. 2 no 2 lit. c from an overall national economic perspective and a regional perspective as well as to assess its readiness for the test phase (para. 2 no. 3) and market readiness (para. 2 no. 4). The FMA shall reach decisions on complete applications for admission to the sandbox taking the opinion into consideration.
		The members of the advisory board (Beirat) are as follows:
		1. a representative of the Federal Ministry of Finance as chairperson,
		2. a representative of the Federal Chancellery (Bundeskanzleramt),
		3. a representative of the FMA,
		4. a representative of the OeNB as well as
		5. up to six other members to be named by the Federal Minister of Finance, who are suitable based on their professional background or other relevant expert knowledge to contribute toward the expert review.
		The members of the advisory board shall perform their function on a voluntary basis. The affairs of the advisor board shall be managed by the Federal Ministry of Finance. All persons who are involved with an opinion shall be obliged to maintain confidentiality about all official, business and trade secrets that have come to their knowledge in the course of their performing this work.
2.	Application of the established operating principles by the entity under the regulatory sandbox, including:	The entity must observe all requirements that are prescribed under law as compulsory in a licensing procedure, such as technical suitability or the requirement that the position is the main occupation for at least one director of a payment service provider under the Payment Services Act 2018 (ZaDiG 2018; Zahlungsdienstegesetz 2018). No provisions are allowed to be suspended in the sandbox, or not to be applied at the discretion of the FMA. Room however remains for the application of proportionality within these legal requirements e.g. a Fit & Proper test for directors. The extent to which the senior management must be fit & proper depends on the scope and nature of the activity during the test phase.
	Potential capital requirements	The legal minimum requirements for granting a license under the respective supervisory act, must also be met for a license in the sandbox. For example, Article 16 para. 1 ZaDiG 2018 stipulates Common Equity Tier 1 of € 125,000.00 for operating a payment instrument business or a payment business. Furthermore, payment institutions are required pursuant to Article 17 para. 1 ZaDiG 2018 to have sufficient own funds at all times. This is dependent on different calculation methods in relation to the nature and scope of the business activity e.g. from the payment volume that flows through the payment institution. For a license, generally substantially higher own funds are required to be held than are compulsory in the provisions on initial capital. To what extent adequate own funds are specifically to be held, is to be evaluated on a case-by-case basis for the test phase. In drawing up the test parameters together with the entity, consideration is given for example whether limited operations with a low number of customers and transactions are initially aimed at. The specific own funds requirement is also based on this factor.
3.	Timeline of sandboxing stages	If all conditions for the application are fully met pursuant to Article 23a para. 2 FMABG and the opinion from the Advisory Board of the Regulatory Sandbox has been received, then the FMA is required to decide about the application within six months.

No.	Area	
		Four stages https://www.fma.gv.at/en/fintech-point-of-contact-sandbox/fma-sandbox/how-it-works/ (in German)
4.	Publicity related to participation in sandbox	Advertising materials of sandbox participants shall not be allowed to create the impression that participation in the sandbox constitutes a benefit for customers. A transparent and non-misleading external appearance is to be observed throughout the entire procedure. It is not possible to advertise the business model using an FMA "seal of quality". It would also be misleading to already offer the prospect of a licence, before one actually exists. The commitment of the sandbox means that both sides must be cautious in dealing with existing reputational risks. Ambiguities or exaggerated reporting are misplaced. The FMA will inform the public about the business model and the sandbox participant prior to the test starting. Operational or trade secrets must be protected.
5.	Application process	An application to be taken up into the sandbox is to be submitted to the FMA. The following conditions shall apply for admission to the sandbox:
		1. For the applicant's sandbox business model, which is based on information and communication technology (ICT):
		a) an assessment as being an activity requiring a license, approval, authorisation or registration in accordance with one of the Federal Acts stated in Article 2 paras. 1 to 4 or pursuant to Regulation (EU) No. 1024/2013 must at least be considered logical or
		b) where a license, approval, authorisation or registration has been granted in accordance with one of the Federal Acts stated in Article 2 paras. 1 to 4, although the applicant may also apply together with an undertaking that is not subject to licensing, approval, authorisation or registration obligations in accordance with one of the Federal Acts stated in Article 2 paras. 1 to 4;
		2. The execution of the sandbox business model:
		a) requires an evaluation by the FMA in accordance with the Federal acts listed in Article 2 paras. 1 to 4, and b) is not subject to exclusive evaluation by the European Central Bank, the Single Resolution Board or a European Supervisory Authority pursuant to Article 21a para. 1 nos. 1 to 4 of this Federal Act, and
		c) is in the economic interests of an innovative financial centre, particularly because of the increased value of innovation, and
		d) is not likely to compromise financial stability or consumer protection;
		3. no general technical or legal impediments exist for the implementation of the business model in the sandbox (readiness for testing purposes), with the exception of the legal conductions to be clarified in the sandbox arising from the respective applicable Federal Acts listed in Article 2 paras. 1 to 4;
		4. it is to be expected that the market readiness of sandbox business models will be accelerated by their being admitted to the sandbox.
		5. It is expected that outstanding issues in relation to supervisory law will be able to be cleared up via the sandbox.
	Application process stages	The FMA may grant a restricted license, approval, authorisation, or registration in accordance with the respective applicable Federal Acts listed in Article 2 paras. 1 to 4 by means of an administrative decision for activities that do not fall under the competence of the European Central Bank, the Single Resolution Board or a European Supervisory Authority pursuant to Article 21a para. 1 nos. 1 to 4. The FMA, without prejudice to other legal provisions therein, may impose appropriate requirements, conditions and time limits.
		At the same time as a restricted licence, approval, authorisation or registration pursuant to para. 5 being granted, or in the case that such permission is not required without unnecessary delay following admission into the sandbox, the FMA, following a hearing of and in cooperation with the participant, shall define the conditions for a test phase including suitable test parameters and measurable targets for evaluating the implementation of the sandbox model.
	Eligibility criteria	To participate, further conditions apply (as per https://technologyquotient.freshfields.com/post/102gbaq/new-regulatory-sandbox-for-austria)
		Innovation – the sandbox business model must be based on information and communication technology. This requirement should be read broadly and in a technology-neutral way. Such innovations include solutions for the (digital or other) transfer, storage and processing of language, text, static and moving images, and data, and will generally cover any activities of fintechs.
		FMA relevance – the sandbox business model must fall within the FMA's authority. For example, business models requiring no authorisation at all or an authorisation for which the FMA is not competent (eg a trade licence) are excluded. Also, if one of the European Central Bank, the Single Resolution Board or a European supervisory authority is the sole competent authority, the business model is not eligible.
		Public interest – the sandbox business model must (especially due to its innovative nature) be in the wider economic interest.
		Acceleration of market maturity – inclusion in the sandbox must accelerate the market maturity of the sandbox business model.
		Test readiness – apart from the regulatory questions to be clarified in the sandbox (see next point), there must

No.	Area	
		be no fundamental technical or legal obstacles to the sandbox business model's implementation.
		Clarification of open regulatory questions – participation in the sandbox must allow for the clarification of open regulatory questions. This excludes any business model that is already authorised by the FMA or on which the FMA has already issued opinions.
		No negative implications – the sandbox business model must not constitute a threat to financial market stability or consumer protection. This requirement was added to the version of the draft bill circulated last year to bring the Austrian sandbox rules further in to line with other countries.
	Application documents	
	Details of acceptance procedure	The participant in the sandbox is an undertaking that the FMA has granted access to the sandbox by means of an administrative decision.
6.	Authorization process, including:	Criteria for admission to the sandbox have been determined and requirements finalised for how the test operates. For example, services that require a licence may never be allowed to be provided "on a test basis" without a licence. The sandbox opens up a new pathway towards a licence for FinTechs, but no "stripped down licence". Supervisory requirements are only adapted within the scope of the principle of proportionality for supervision depending the business model, where supervisory laws permit this.
		In case of activities that are of limited-scale and scope, the FMA may grant a restricted license or authorisation, as already stipulated in the applicable legislation, by means of an administrative decision. However, such restricted license may be granted only for activities that do not fall under the competence of the European Central Bank, the Single Resolution Board or a European Supervisory Authority.
	List of documents and information required for the license application, conditions included in the license	The applicants shall submit to the FMA all necessary documents, especially business plans, for evaluation of the criteria [of application process] in nos. 1 and 2, provide it with information and to submit proof to it. The conditions pursuant to no. 2 lit. c being fulfilled is to be substantiated separately by the applicant. Furthermore, the applicant shall also submit a justified explanation, in which from their perspective readiness for testing purposes pursuant to no. 3 exists. The applicant must substantiate the requirement pursuant to no. 4 and specify the questions pursuant to no. 5 as specifically as possible.
		The FMA shall make the Federal Minister of Finance aware of applications pursuant to para. 2, that are complete except for the opinion that is required to be obtained.
		During participation, participants must provide information to the FMA upon request, submit documents, and provide access to the information and communications technology (ICT) underlying the business model. This obligation to cooperate exists where it is necessary for the assessment of the activity conducted by the participant under supervisory law, and irrespective of other obligations applicable for the participation based on the Federal Acts listed in Article 2 paras. 1 to 4.
7.	Resources	
	Any financial assistance given to the FinTechs	No
	Fees related to application/participation in the sandbox	No fees arise during the process for admittance. Fees arise in the case of administrative decisions being issued – and are based upon the FMA's standard charge rates, especially for an administrative decision granting a licence.
		The fees pursuant to Article 19 para. 10 for the granting of the licence, approval, authorisation and registration pursuant to para. 5 are to be borne by the entity itself. (article 10: For the authorisation of situations in accordance with fee items 44 and 45 and 50 to 59 of the Regulation on Federal Administration Fees 1983 (BVwAbgV – Bundesverwaltungsabgabenverordnung) as published in Federal Law Gazette No. 24/1983, in the version published in Federal Law Gazette II No. 146/2000, instead of federal administration fees, authorisation fees are to be paid to the FMA in accordance with the Regulation on Fees (Gebührenverordnung) to be issued by the FMA. This shall also apply to official acts pursuant to the fee items 1 to 5, provided that these official acts fall within the responsibility of the FMA. The fees may not exceed the average costs arising from the authorization or other official acts, taking a share of the fixed costs into account. The authorisation fees shall be assigned in the respective accounting group with the aim of reducing costs taking into account the subaccounting groups in the respective cost provisions of the laws listed in Article 2; more detailed rules shall be determined about its execution in the regulation to be issued pursuant to para. 7.)
	Resources on the part of the regulator	The government allocates a ring-fenced contribution of EUR 500 000 per financial year to finance the sandbox that is to be used by the FMA for the running costs of the sandbox. Directly attributable personnel and material expenses incurred by FMA within the scope of the assessment of the sandbox
		suitability pursuant to para. 2, the development of targets and test parameters pursuant to para. 6 and the reports to the Federal Minister of Finance pursuant to para. 7 shall be covered exclusively by this contribution by the Federal Government. The costs of the sandbox in this regard shall not be allocated to the accounting groups pursuant to Article 19 para. 1. Any immaterial shortfall of up to a maximum of 5% per FMA financial year of the ring-fenced amount according to the first sentence is excluded from this amount. Such an immaterial shortfall is to be broken down into the individual accounting groups using the ratio pursuant to Article 19 para. 2. Any surplus shall be allocated to a provision.

No.	Area	
8.	Sandbox testing phase (including dedicated regulatory guidance)	a) Admission, b) Pre-Support, c) Sandbox Test and d) Evaluation Phase. During the admission phase, the applicant submits their application that is reviewed by the FMA and the Regulatory Sandbox Advisory Board (Beirat). During the presupport phase, eligible participants work closely with the FMA to decide upon test duration, the KPIs to be monitored, and discuss any potential restrictions / conditions attached to the license. In addition, during this phase a licensing procedure is conducted with an unlicensed or registered FinTech. In the case of an incumbent market participant a decision may potentially be required regarding an extension of the existing license.
		Once the financial market participant enters the Sandbox Test phase, the testing parameters and milestones that were agreed upon during the Pre-Support phase, will be regularly discussed in the management meetings with the FMA. During the final Evaluation step in the process, the outcomes of the test phase are evaluated, the business model exits the sandbox and is transferred to regular supervision.
9.	End of the sandbox tests/ Exit procedure	The entity may request to exit the sandbox at any time, and the evaluation and exit phase 4 of the sandbox is then initiated.
		Participation is to be limited to a period of a maximum of two years in accordance with the requirements of the sandbox business model.
		The FMA shall end sandbox participation either at the participant's request or by its own initiative, where the conditions for participation cease to exist, where it is accepted that the desired purpose of participation in the sandbox may not be achieved, or after the end of two years.
10.	Rules of supervision of the entities conducting activity in the regulatory sandbox, including	The FMA shall report to the Federal Minister of Finance in writing on a quarterly basis about the developments within the sandbox. The Federal Minister of Finance shall also make these reports available to the advisory board established pursuant to para. 3. Moreover, the FMA shall at the request
		of the Federal Minister of Finance provide information about the sandbox and its participants in order to permit the evaluation of the overall national economic perspective or regional perspective of sandbox business models pursuant to para. 3
11.	Other aspects related to conducting business that are useful and reasonable for the proper implementation of the regulatory sandbox, including:	
	Issues related to the legal form of the entity, owners	The Article 23a of FMABG does not specify required legal form of the entity.
	The period of operations carried out so far	There is no specific regulation in the frame of the sandbox.
	Participation in the compensation system	There is no specific regulation in the frame of the sandbox.
	Protection of intellectual property	There is no specific regulation in the frame of the sandbox.
	Requirements related to compliance with AML requirements	There is no specific regulation in the frame of the sandbox.
	Privacy protection	There is no specific regulation in the frame of the sandbox.
12.	Did the introduced solutions support the development of Fintech, including:	
	How many firms participated? What was the approval rate?	Eight FinTechs have been admitted to the FMA Regulatory Sandbox so far. Five of these providers are targeting an authorisation as European Crowdfunding Service Providers in accordance with the EU Crowdfunding Regulation. The other three intend to conduct innovative financial services in relation to crypto assets and financial instruments in such a way that requires a license under the Securities Supervision Act 2018 or the Austrian Banking Act.[1] To date, there is no information on the number of refused applicants.
	Whether they were encouraging for the innovative entities to enter the regulatory sandbox	FMA sandbox clearly communicates its design to attract applicants and set up realistic expectations on its operation.
	Have they ensured the safety of entities using	Services that require a license may never be allowed to be provided without a license. The sandbox maintains a standard level of consumer protection on the Austrian financial market.

No.	Area	
	the services of regulatory sandbox participants?	

Note:
1. FMA's Regulatory Sandbox presents positive results: eight FinTechs already on their way to regulatory market maturity, one has already obtained a licence https://www.fma.gv.at/en/fmas-regulatory-sandbox-presents-positive-results-eight-fintechs-already-on-their-way-to-regulatory-market-maturity-one-has-already-obtained-a-licence/
Source: FMA; OECD research.

Table A D.2. Slovakian sandbox

No.	Area	
1.	Institution(s) involved in the selection of participants and the operation of the sandbox	National Bank of Slovakia
2.	Application of the established operating principles by the entity under the regulatory sandbox, including:	The legislative requirements applicable to the entity from the existing regulations during the whole sandboxing period.
	conduct of business rules	There are not any sandbox specific conduct of business rules. Companies must adhere to existing Slovak regulation, which is based on European legislation.
	technical and operational requirements	The Operational Rules of the regulatory sandbox[1] consider financial innovation to be a financial product, service, or business model which due to the innovative application of technology may considerably affect the functioning of the Slovak financial market.
	potential capital requirements	The sandbox requires participants to have a license to enter the testing phase. Sandbox does not waive or alter any capital requirements in place related to the licensing process.
3.	Timeline of sandbox stages	Application Assessment – up to 2 months Preparation – 6 months with a possibility to extend Testing – 6 months with a possibility to extend Exit - 1 month
4.	Publicity related to participation in sandbox	Within three working days after the start of the testing phase, the NBS will publish on its website the business name of the participant (if the participant is a service provider, also the business name of the supervised entity with its consent with participation in the sandbox), the date of entry of the participant into the regulatory sandbox, a brief description of the tested financial innovation. The information remains published also after the end of texting. Upon exit, it is specified that the testing period has ended.
5.	Application process	
	Application process stages	Sandbox is not operated on a cohort basis, interested entities are encouraged to apply anytime. The application process is as follows[2]: • The applicant delivers the application to the NBS (in paper or electronic form). • The NBS will confirm the delivery and will assess its formal and content requirements. The NBS may call on the applicant to eliminate shortcomings or supplement the application within a reasonable time. • The NBS will plan a meeting with the applicant to learn more detailed information regarding the applicant and the scheduled testing. The NBS will notify the applicant **within two months** from the date of delivery of the complete application whether it will allow him to enter into the regulatory sandbox; the time limit does not apply to the entity interested in cross-border testing. If the NBS notifies the applicant that it does not allow him to enter into the regulatory sandbox, the applicant may submit another application no earlier than **6 months** from the date of delivery of this notification.
	Eligibility criteria	A participant in the regulatory sandbox may be:[3] • the supervised entity (an entity supervised by NBS pursuant to legislation[4]), • the foreign supervised entity (an entity supervised by a foreign financial market supervisory authority in another Member State of the European Union), • the applicant for authorisation (the applicant for authorisation a natural or legal person who has applied for authorisation or for other permission to perform activities

No.	Area	
		or for registration pursuant to legislation[5]), • the service provider (the service provider a third party who, based on an outsourcing agreement concluded with the supervised entity, applies a procedure, provides a service, or performs an activity or part thereof for which the supervised • entity is authorised according to legislation[5]), • the future supervised entity (the future supervised entity an entity performing activities that will be subject to legislation within the competence of the NBS, which was published in the Collection of Laws of the Slovak Republic or in the Official Journal of the European Union but has not yet entered into force or is not yet applicable). **Further evaluation criteria[6]** • Applicant is to be of a good repute, • the subject of the consultations is the application of legislation within the competence of the NBS[7] • can demonstrate its readiness to participate in the regulatory sandbox and readiness of financial innovation for testing • there is the need for testing • it is innovative • it has positive impacts on clients in the Slovak financial market and the absence of significant negative impacts on financial stability in the Slovak Republic. The NBS assesses the fulfillment of all these criteria according to the Methodology for the assessment of the criteria to enter into the regulatory sandbox.
	Application documents	A detailed set of information and documents required for the applicant shall attach to the application form, which is available in Annex 1 of the Operating Rules of the regulatory sandbox. The application consists of the following parts: • Information about the applicant • Information about financial innovation • Preparatory phase and testing • Declaration of honor • Consent to the processing of personal data • Familiarisation with the Operating rules of the regulatory sandbox applicable from 1 January 2022
	Details of acceptance procedure	NBS recognizes possible limits of its capacity. If there are several applicants who meet the conditions for participation and the capacity of the sandbox is on its limits, the NBS may postpone the entry of the new participant accordingly.[8] Upon receiving and evaluating application, successful applicant becomes participant of the **Preparatory phase[9]**, which consists of consultations aiming to: enable the participant to have consultations with the NBS, which should help the participant to adjust financial innovation in compliance with the legislation within the competence of the NBS to determine the course of the testing phase in the form of a testing plan. Following the consultations in the preparatory phase, the NBS will ask the participant to submit a draft testing plan within the specified time limit.[10] The preparatory phase lasts a maximum of 6 months. At the request of the participant, the NBS may extend it accordingly.
6.	Authorization process, including:	
	List of documents and information required for the license application, conditions included in the license	The list of documents varies considerably depending on kind of service provided, as there is number of licenses by NBS.
	Refusal and withdrawal of licenses for entities operating under a regulatory sandbox (non – EU countries - as long as the business activity is supervised both in the scope of the EU law and the law of non - EU country)	It is key characteristic of the sandbox, that if the participant is the applicant for authorisation, that participant must obtain the relevant authorisation during the preparatory phase. The participant may test financial innovation in the regulatory sandbox only after obtaining the relevant authorisation.[11] If the participant is the applicant for authorisation, the licensing procedure takes place independently of the preparatory phase of the regulatory sandbox. If the participant does not obtain the relevant authorisation by the time of submission of the draft testing plan, the testing plan must stipulate that testing can only start after the authorisation has been granted. Termination of participation is sandbox is not directly connected to license of the entity.
7.	Resources	
	Financial assistance given to the FinTechs	Not provided

No.	Area	
	Fees related to application/participation in the sandbox	There is not a fee connected with participation in the sandbox. However, the entity must be licensed to enter testing stage, which carries considerable costs given needed legal expertise.
	Resources on the part of the regulator	There are not officers dedicated only to operation of sandbox, operation of sandbox is part of their agenda and officers are involved based on the expertise needed. Board of the sandbox consist of directors of relevant departments of NBS.
8.	Data pool or data infrastructure provided to the participants	The sandbox does not provide data functionalities at this point. The consultation prior establishment of the sandbox considered testing of innovations related to data in virtual sandbox[12], but the respondents did not express strong demand for it.[13]
9.	Sandbox testing phase (including dedicated regulatory guidance)	The testing refers to the implementation of financial innovation on the Slovak financial market in accordance with the testing plan.[14] The aim of the testing phase is the implementation of the tested financial innovation on the Slovak financial market in accordance with the testing plan.[15] Testing of financial innovation does not affect the obligations imposed on the participant by legislation. **Process of testing:** • The testing plan shall set a period for testing, which shall not exceed 6 months. • The participant informs the NBS in advance of the intention to suspend or prematurely terminate the testing on its own initiative. • Communication between participant and NBS: • The participant shall continuously inform the NBS about the course of testing in accordance with the testing plan. • Regardless of the testing plan, the participant immediately informs the NBS about serious problems, unexpected situations, or other facts that could have a significant impact on the testing process. The NBS may call on the participant to remedy the problem within the specified time limit. If the participant does not remedy the problem within the specified time limit, the NBS will prematurely terminate the participant's participation in the regulatory sandbox. • The NBS may request additional information from the participant on the course of testing at any time. • At the participant's request, the NBS may provide consultations to the participant during the testing phase. • Adherence to the testing plan: • If the participant does not comply with the testing plan, the NBS will ask him for an explanation within the specified time limit and at the same time inform him that the NBS may prematurely terminate the participant's participation in the regulatory sandbox. • If the participant does not provide an explanation and does not remedy the problem within the specified time limit, the NBS will prematurely terminate the participant's participation in the regulatory sandbox. **Changes of testing plan**: • The participant may request the NBS to change the testing plan. • Until the NBS approves the change in the testing plan, the participant proceeds according to the originally approved testing plan. • The NBS may send comments to the participant on the request to change the testing plan and set a time limit for the comments to be incorporated. • If the participant does not incorporate NBS' comments within the specified time limit or the NBS does not agree with the change of the testing plan, the NBS notifies the participant that its request has not been approved and that if it is still interested in continuing testing, it is obliged to comply with the approved testing plan. • If the NBS approves the change, it will immediately notify the participant. **Extension of testing period**: In justified cases, the participant may request the NBS to extend the testing period by a maximum of **6 months**.
10.	End of the sandbox tests / Exit procedure	**Scheduled termination:** Final report:[16] Within **one month** after the end of the testing, the participant shall deliver to the NBS the final report stating in particular: • a summary of the testing, • an evaluation of whether the expected test results have been achieved, • problems and unexpected situations that occurred during testing, • whether the participant intends to continue offering financial innovation to clients

No.	Area	
		upon the termination of its participation in the regulatory sandbox. **Final meeting**[17]: • Within one month from the delivery of the final report, the NBS will organize a final meeting with the participant to discuss the final report and the course of the participant's participation in the regulatory sandbox. • The NBS may replace the final meeting with a written statement on the final report. • Participation in the regulatory sandbox is terminated on the day of the final meeting or on the day of delivery of the NBS' written statement on the final report. **Premature termination**[18]**:** NBS may prematurely terminate the participant's participation in the regulatory sandbox, in case that a participant: • does not follow the instructions of the NBS, • does not remedy identified shortcomings even after a request from the NBS. The participant in the regulatory sandbox is obliged to notify their clients that their participation in the regulatory sandbox is expiring and the provision of the product/service will no longer be subject to the previously communicated restrictions.
11.	Rules of supervision of the entities conducting activity in the regulatory sandbox, including carrying out a potential inspection	The sandbox does not provide for a waiver or alteration from the general inspection powers. In its consultation material envisioning possible functioning of Slovak sandbox prior its establishment, NBS wrote about necessity of proportional approach to sanctions for participants in the regulatory sandbox. It noted that given the close cooperation of the entity with NBS, the participant following all the instructions from NBS is not likely to violation of legal rules and thus the participant should not face any sanctions from NBS. However, it noted that if a participant in the regulatory sandbox nevertheless engages in sanctionable conduct, NBS will apply the relevant sanctions proportionately within the limits of legal regulations. In case that the legal rules allow it, NBS may initially refrain from imposing a penalty and give the participant the opportunity to remedy the deficiency.[19] The topic was not revisited by NBS after setting up the sandbox, and there not have been participants breaking the rules to see case study of the reaction.
12.	Other aspects related to conducting business that are useful and reasonable for the proper implementation of the regulatory sandbox, including:	
	issues related to the legal form of the entity, owners	Applicants can be any legal person. The rules imply that individual can apply. However only licensed company can enter testing phase.
	The period of operations carried out so far	There is not specific requirement.
	participation in the compensation system	This is not applicable.
	protection of intellectual property	The sandbox does not give participants any distinct intellectual property protection in relation to other entities.
	requirements related to compliance with AML requirements	The sandbox does not waive or alter general requirements.
	Privacy protection	The sandbox does not waive or alter general requirements.
13.	Did the introduced solutions support the development of Fintech, including:	
	How many firms participated? What was the approval rate?	There is not information about any firm reaching the testing phase yet.
	whether they were encouraging for the innovative entities to enter the regulatory sandbox	NBS has network of contacts on relevant stakeholders thanks to its activities in Innovation hub. NBS widely disseminated the news of the sandbox among Slovak public, who also had a chance to contribute to the consultation regarding the design of the sandbox prior its establishment. There is no participant in testing phase yet and it has one participant so far, there is no information on refused applicants.
	Have they ensured the safety of entities using the services of regulatory sandbox participants?	Given that there is no waiver or alteration of general regulation, there is no risk arising from that. The safety is strengthened by intense exchange of knowledge among NBS and entity using the sandbox, which enables NBS to identify possible risks arising from the innovative model. The regulator and the participant maintain a close dialogue throughout the process, which ensures a robust knowledge exchange between the two parties regarding the regulatory process and the participant's activity.

Notes:
1. Operating rules of the regulatory sandbox, Article 3, Letter e
2. Operating rules of the regulatory sandbox, Chapter V
3. Operating rules of the regulatory sandbox, Chapter II, Article 4
4. E. g. Act No. 747/2004 Coll, as amended
5. E. g. Act No. 310/1992 Coll., Home Savings Act, as amended, Act No. 483/2001 Coll., on Banks and on amendments and supplements to certain laws, as amended, Act No. 566/2001 Coll, on Securities and Investment Services (The Securities Act) and on amendments and supplements to certain laws, as amended, Act No. 43/2004 Coll, on the Old-Age Pension Saving Scheme and on amendments and supplements to certain laws, as amended, Act No. 650/2004 Coll., on the Supplementary Pension Scheme and on amendments to certain laws, as amended, Act No. 747/2004 Coll., as amended
6. Operating rules of the regulatory sandbox, Chapters III and IV
7. Consultations provide non-binding opinion by the NBS clarifying the application of legislation within the competence of the NBS, which is applicable to the participant and to its tested activities
8. Operating rules of the regulatory sandbox, Chapter II, Article 8
9. Operating rules of the regulatory sandbox, Chapter VI
10. Particular parts of testing plan are specified by Operating rules of the regulatory sandbox, Chapter VI, Article 21
11. Particular parts of testing plan are specified by Operating rules of the regulatory sandbox, Chapter VI, Articles 24 – 26
12. Regulatory sandbox consultation document, Chapter 1.5, Other types of sandbox
13. Vyhodnotenie konzultácie k regulačnému sandbox, page 7
14. OR Article 3, Letter f
15. OR Chapter VII
16. OR Chapter VIII, Article 38
17. OR Chapter VIII, Article 39
18. OR Chapter VIII, Article 41 – 43
19. regulatory sandbox | consultation document | June 2020, page 14.
Source: NBS; OECD research.

Table A D.3. UK sandbox

No.	Area	
1.	Institution(s) involved in the selection of participants and the operation of the sandbox	The Financial Conduct Authority (FCA) -
2.	Application of the established operating principles by the entity under the regulatory sandbox, including:	
	conduct of business rules	The conduct of business guidelines in the FCA regulatory sandbox are intended to make sure that businesses taking part in the sandbox are conducting themselves in a fair, open, and organised manner. These regulations aim to safeguard consumers from harm and encourage market competition. Through its Handbook of rules and guidance, the FCA develops the business behaviour guidelines for companies taking part in the regulatory sandbox. The Handbook defines the FCA's requirements for firms to comply with these laws and provides firms with information on how to do business. Depending on the nature of the business, specific standards that organisations must follow may include those relating to customer fairness, disclosure, and transparency.
		Firms are expected to have sufficient systems and controls in place to ensure compliance with conduct of business regulations in the FCA regulatory sandbox and to be able to provide the FCA with proof of this upon request. Additionally, businesses must have a procedure in place for managing complaints and submit any significant complaints to the FCA. Moreover, the FCA may mandate that companies submit to routine supervisory visits and submit to regular reports on their business operations. In order to safeguard consumers and foster competition, the FCA may also impose extra conduct of business criteria on companies taking part in the sandbox as it sees right.
	technical and operational requirements	The FCA continuously updates the operational requirements, and firms are expected to comply with the latest guidance and rules at all times.
	potential capital requirements	There is no need to be capitalised before applying for sandbox or before applying for authorisation. However, firms need to satisfy FCA Authorisations team that they can get sufficient funding, and will need to capitalise the firm before final authorization can be granted. Required capitalisation will vary depending on the actual business model. Firms may wish to start the process of getting a business bank account well in advance of applying for authorisation. (page 11)
3.	Timeline of sandbox stages	The sandbox typically consists of several stages, including a pre-application stage, an application stage,

No.	Area	
		and a testing stage, during which the FCA works closely with the participating companies to ensure compliance with regulatory requirements and to mitigate any potential risks to consumers. The FCA has also published guidance on its website that provides information on how to apply to the sandbox and what to expect during the testing phase. The specifics of the sandbox stages change over time, as the FCA is constantly adapting and improving the program based on feedback and lessons learned.
4.	Publicity related to participation in sandbox	e.g. *What is published regarding the participants of sandbox and when? Are there regular reports or ad hoc press releases?*
		Is there limit on using participation as PR?
5.	Application process	https://www.fca.org.uk/publication/fca/fca-regulatory-sandbox-guide.pdf
	Application process stages	p.6, https://www.fca.org.uk/publication/fca/fca-regulatory-sandbox-guide.pdf
	Eligibility criteria	In **scope** - Innovation intended for UK market; relevant activity is regulated
		Genuine innovation - Desk research produces no comparable examples; innovation is clear step-in-change
		Consumer benefit – Innovation is likely to benefit consumers; potential risks have been assessed; innovation will make entry or compliance FCA rules easier
		Readiness – there is a well-developed testing plan
		Need for innovation support – There is a genuine need to test the innovation in the sandbox (innovation does not fit the regulatory framework, or full process would be too costly)
		https://www.fca.org.uk/publication/fca/fca-regulatory-sandbox-eligibility-criteria.pdf
	Application documents	https://www.fca.org.uk/publication/fca/regulatory-sandbox-application-form-guidance.pdf
		Assessment of process:
		Having an external industry panel of experts provide their opinion on what was genuinely innovative and commercially viable was valuable in making accurate assessments of which proposals were supported.
		The platform features worked well for the online application portal and enabled efficiency gains compared with other previous application systems used for FCA innovation services.
		The application process was not subject to the same level of scrutiny and rigour as Regulatory Sandbox applications. This is appropriate on the basis that digital sandbox participants represent a significantly lower risk of harm, given that tests are conducted. Source: page 25 https://www.fca.org.uk/publication/corporate/digital-sandbox-joint-report.pdf
6.	Resources	
	Financial assistance given to the FinTechs	
	Fees related to application/participation in the sandbox	There is no charge for applying for or being accepted into the sandbox, or for any of Innovate's services. However, firms that need to be authorised or registered, including conducting their sandbox test, will need to pay the standard authorisation or registration fee. More information on fees can be found on their website. The fees for full authorisation are the same as the fees for restricted authorisation. (page 11 https://www.fca.org.uk/publication/fca/fca-regulatory-sandbox-guide.pdf)
	Resources on the part of the regulator	
7.	Data pool or data infrastructure provided to the participants	
		Access to synthetic data was identified as the most important feature by far, by most participants (92% ranked data or Juptyer as the highest expected use). However, the average 'rating' of the utility of the data was 5/10 (this also includes additional data sets outside of synthetic data).
		For most teams, data did not fully meet their needs. As noted in the use cases recommendations, the sheer breadth of the required data across 3 different domains meant that there was a trade-off between volume and quality.
		It is important to recognise that synthetic data is a nascent and enormously complex field. Even with world-leading expertise contributed by the Turing Institute, the Working Group was unable to create the required richness across so many data sets.
		Feedback also indicated that better data documentation was needed at the outset of the pilot to avoid resources being required to answer participants' data questions. This documentation should:
		• Provide clear descriptions of how the synthetic data was modelled, eg what typologies exist, in what ways is it representative of real data. • Give an understanding of which data sets are linked to each other. • Be published before teams apply. Teams had unclear data expectations going into the pilot while writing applications which contributed to the misalignment of expectations and teams

No.	Area	
		having to pivot solutions.
		Many teams would have preferred full access to data outside of the platform, for example via S3 buckets. The IDE limited teams to a certain number of calls per day and they could not ingest data onto their own platform. Allowing this approach would also reduce the cost of computing ie the cloud credits required to be provided by the Working Group.
		However, ring fencing data assets behind the IDE enabled the monitoring of usage, prevented data leakage and ensured sustained engagement with the pilot. This contributed to the development of a supporting ecosystem for participants.
		Feedback from participants and observers (particularly financial institutions as potential customers of the solutions) indicated that synthetic data can only enable product validation if the synthetic data assets are commonly understood and recognised by industry - otherwise they are more limited to serving a role in PoC and product development. Industry participants can't evaluate the effectiveness of potential solutions if the input is not understood at a technical level. Source: https://www.fca.org.uk/publication/corporate/digital-sandbox-joint-report.pdf

Source: FCA, OECD research.

www.ingramcontent.com/pod-product-compliance
Ingram Content Group UK Ltd.
Pitfield, Milton Keynes, MK11 3LW, UK
UKHW051507290926
15471UKWH00008B/1472

9 789264 504240